What teachers need to know about Spelling

PETER WESTWOOD

ACER Press

First published 2008
by ACER Press, an imprint of
Australian Council for Educational Research Ltd
19 Prospect Hill Road, Camberwell
Victoria, 3124, Australia

www.acerpress.com.au
sales@acer.edu.au

Text © Peter Westwood 2008
Design and typography © ACER Press 2008

This book is copyright. All rights reserved. Except under the conditions described in the *Copyright Act 1968* of Australia and subsequent amendments, and any exceptions permitted under the current statutory licence scheme administered by Copyright Agency Limited (www.copyright.com.au), no part of this publication may be reproduced, stored in a retrieval system, transmitted, broadcast or communicated in any form or by any means, optical, digital, electronic, mechanical, photocopying, recording or otherwise, without the written permission of the publisher.

Edited by Carolyn Glascodine
Cover and text design by Mary Mason
Typeset by Mary Mason
Printed in Australia by Ligare

National Library of Australia Cataloguing-in-Publication data:

Author:	Westwood, Peter S. (Peter Stuart), 1936–
Title:	What teachers need to know about spelling / Peter Westwood.
Publisher:	Camberwell, Vic. : ACER Press, 2008.
ISBN:	9780864319449 (pbk.)
Notes:	Includes index.
	Bibliography.
Subjects:	Spelling—Study and teaching.
Dewey Number:	372.632

Contents

Preface — vii

1 Where is spelling on the literacy agenda? — 1
Public interest in spelling — 2
Government initiatives — 4
Current situation — 6
Teachers' expertise — 8

2 The anatomy of spelling — 10
Sub-skills and processes in spelling — 11
The reading–spelling connection — 17
The spelling–handwriting connection — 19

3 Developmental and strategic aspects of spelling — 21
Stages in spelling development — 22
Beyond stage theory — 24
Strategies for spelling — 25
The importance of teaching effective strategies for spelling — 28

4 General issues in teaching spelling — 34
School policy and cross-curricular aspects — 35
Spelling in the primary school — 36
Spelling in secondary schools — 41
Arousing students' interest in words — 41
Assistive technology — 43

5 Activities for teaching and learning — 46
Developing students' awareness of spelling principles and components — 47
Word study — 49
Explicit teaching of spelling strategies — 53

	Proofreading and error correction	55
	Mastering a core of high-frequency words	56
6	**Intervention for spelling difficulties**	**59**
	Possible causes of difficulty	60
	Intervention: basic principles	63
	Research on spelling interventions	64
	Specific interventions for weak spellers	65
	Peer support	70
7	**Assessing spelling skills and strategies**	**72**
	Purposes of assessment	73
	Methods of assessment	74
	Self-assessment	78
	Additional resources	79

Appendices — 81

Appendix 1: A core list of priority words — 81
Appendix 2: Some predictable spelling patterns — 82
Appendix 3: Simple word building — 84
Appendix 4: Word families: two examples — 85
Appendix 5: Word sorts: an example — 86

References — 87
Index — 101

Teacher – trying to spell is simply crazy –
With rules that are fuzzy and logic that's hazy.
Teacher – why doesn't s-e-d spell said,
When b-e-d spells bed and r-e-d spells red?

Rowell (2007) *Spelling woes*, p. 336.

Preface

Spelling is not taught effectively in many schools. An enormous gap exists between current research knowledge about spelling and contemporary classroom practice. Studies in the past two decades have revealed much about the normal development of spelling ability and how students can be helped most effectively to become proficient spellers. Research has also explored the many causes of spelling difficulty and disability. Unfortunately, many teachers remain ignorant of much of this information because the topic of spelling rarely features in any significant way in pre-service and in-service teacher education programs. When it does gain a mention it is usually dealt with from a discredited whole-language perspective that favours informality rather than direct instruction.

As I indicate in several places in this book, teachers remain confused about their role in relation to spelling instruction; and they often leave students' spelling skills to develop incidentally. Teachers' own knowledge of spelling principles and spelling strategies is often lacking in depth, so they are uncertain precisely what needs to be taught and how to teach it, even if they have the desire to give spelling greater prominence in their literacy program.

This book attempts to bridge the gap between knowledge that has accumulated from research on spelling acquisition and the practicalities of teaching spelling more effectively in schools. I have devoted some attention to current trends and community views on the importance (or otherwise) of spelling standards because this provides the context in which change is now beginning to occur, partly as a result of a call for greater accountability for students' educational progress.

I have addressed developmental aspects of spelling, together with the need to teach students effective strategies for analysing and encoding words. Practical suggestions have been included for methods and activities that are applicable for all students, and this is supplemented by specific advice on assessment of spelling and helping weaker spellers. Links to other sources of information are provided in each chapter and additional material appears in the appendices. This book presents a concise summary of what teachers need to know about students' spelling, and how best to support its development.

My sincere thanks go to Carolyn Glascodine and Maureen O'Keefe for their efficient editing and management of the original manuscript. My sincere thanks also to the staff at ACER Press for their professional support.

PETER WESTWOOD

RESOURCES www.acer.edu.au/need2know

Readers may access the online resources mentioned throughout this book through direct links at www.acer.edu.au/need2know

one

Where is spelling on the literacy agenda?

KEY ISSUES

- Public interest in spelling standards remains very strong.
- Parents are concerned that schools do not seem to take a sufficiently active role in teaching children to spell.
- Official views have swung back in favour of systematic instruction.
- Guidelines and policies have been developed; but teachers remain uncertain about how best to teach spelling.
- There is little evidence that teacher education courses are providing beginning teachers with adequate guidance on instructional methods for spelling.

After many years of almost total neglect, the teaching of spelling is now receiving more attention in curriculum policy and assessment documents, in the media, and in educational research. Several writers have observed that for the previous 30 years the education system increasingly de-emphasised formal spelling instruction in schools in favour of an incidental approach to learning (e.g., Egan & van Gorder, 1998; Foorman et al., 2006; Griffiths, 2004; Wallace, 2006). This trend had left teachers of literacy confused about their precise role in relation to students' spelling development (Bryan, 2003; Fresch, 2007; Johnson, 2001; Kervin & McKenzie, 2005; Louden & Rohl, 2006). For example, teachers wonder if they should devote specific time and attention to teaching spelling in a systematic manner, or should they deal with spelling only through corrective feedback on students' written work? If they are to adopt a systematic approach, what corpus of words should they attempt to teach and how should they attempt to teach the words? Should they encourage memorisation of spelling patterns or should they teach students to apply particular strategies for learning and remembering words? Should they encourage students to invent the spelling of words they wish to use rather than worrying about accuracy? Are spelling lists useful? What purpose is served by regularly testing students' spelling? These, and many other issues, still appear to cause teachers some degree of anxiety (Kervin & McKenzie, 2005; Templeton & Morris, 1999).

Public interest in spelling

Naturally, spelling is a topic that attracts interest among the general public. Vedora and Stromer (2007, p. 489) observe that, 'Spelling is a vital part of the educational process because learning to read, write, spell and express one's thoughts accurately in writing is essential for a literate society'.

It is often felt (rightly or wrongly) that the standard of an individual's spelling is some indication of his or her intelligence, ability and level of education. Employers expect their employees to be able to spell if their job calls for communication in writing. Entry to tertiary courses of study frequently calls for written application and often a supplementary written test. The standard of an applicant's spelling is one factor that could influence any decision made by a selection panel. Even writing letters and emails to friends can be a source of embarrassment if they contain glaring errors that are later identified. As Templeton and Morris (1999, p. 102) remark, 'Spelling is so visible, so obvious, that it often assumes the role of a proxy for literacy and in that role is bound to generate controversy'.

Parents represent one group with very strong views about spelling. They expect schools to regard accurate spelling as important, and to develop their children's spelling proficiency. They become worried, for example, when their children take written work home from school containing 'invented' spelling and no evidence that the teacher has provided guidance or corrections. Teachers probably spend much time and effort trying to convince parents that allowing young children to invent the spelling of words they wanted to use will not cause long-term problems (Kolodziej & Columba, 2005). Many parents remain unconvinced.

Parents' concern seemed justified in 1994 when a study in South Australia revealed a significant decline in primary school students' spelling standards since 1978 – covering a period in the 1980s and early 1990s in which whole-language philosophy permeated almost all classroom literacy practices in that state (Westwood, 1994). When the results were released, public interest was very great indeed, with regular features and letters to the editor in the press, and interviews on television. To provide some evidence of this public concern, condensed extracts from two typical letters to the editor of the Adelaide daily newspaper *The Advertiser* of 12 April 1994 are presented here:

> Are children being encouraged to invent their spelling and then left to discover the correct spelling later? To encourage young children to use and spell experimentally words within their vocabulary but outside their spelling range is sound practice but surely there should be a stage in their education when formal grammar and spelling lessons are introduced to discipline their earlier freedom. Our language is too precious, too precise, too flexible, too elegant, to be left to casual instruction.
>
> D.B., Eden Hills

> [Good practice] should be that when a child is learning to read and write at primary school level that the student is taught to do this correctly from the beginning. The idea that 'don't worry about the spelling, this will come later' does not work for all the children and the inability to spell can reflect in lack of reading skills also. Hence, by high school age, some students are still not able to read and write to a satisfactory standard, and without these skills other subjects are jeopardised.
>
> D.W., Parent Liaison, Salisbury High School

Of course, advocates and disciples of whole language hit back. For example, in the same issue of *The Advertiser* (12 April 1994) a university language arts lecturer criticised the research findings, saying:

> First, the survey itself takes spelling out of the context in which it matters – writing. Second, children's spelling achievement is seen as indicative of literacy standards. We all know that there is a lot more to being literate than spelling correctly! Third, tenuous and unsubstantiated connections are drawn between current teaching methodologies and spelling results as

measured in a test ... [and] the invidious idea that the instantaneous correct spelling of words should be the goal of schooling is reinforced. While this is a useful skill, the ability to recognise errors in writing and to correct them with a dictionary is eminently preferable.

L.W., Flinders University of South Australia

It is not surprising that spelling instruction has been noted as a flashpoint in the heated debates over the merits of whole-language-oriented teaching and more structured approaches (Templeton & Morris, 1999). The so-called 'reading wars' between exponents of opposing philosophies actually includes battles and skirmishes related specifically to spelling instruction.

Perhaps it is important to explain at this point that in the early 1980s teachers in South Australia had been greatly influenced by the in-service professional training program known as ELIC (Early Literacy In-service Course). During that time, as a result of advice disseminated through ELIC, there was a very rapid reduction in the amount of time teachers devoted to the explicit teaching of spelling and phonics. Instead, these component skills were to be taught only in context; in other words, spelling was to be addressed as an integral part of the writing process. Whole-language principles dictated that decontextualised instruction of component skills is undesirable. It was firmly believed that students would become proficient spellers in a 'natural' way if they simply had the opportunity to write every day about meaningful topics and received corrective feedback from their teachers.

The notion of 'natural learning' is attractive, but Graham (2000) has argued strongly that this approach, if used alone, is inadequate for effective spelling development. The data from the South Australian study appear to support this view, particularly since a follow-up study in 2004 showed an improvement in spelling standards when whole-language teaching gave way in the late 1990s to a more balanced approach that embodied some explicit teaching (Westwood & Bissaker, 2005).

Government initiatives

During the 1990s, growing concern was expressed that too many students in Australia (for example, almost 30 per cent of students in Years 3 and 5) were not achieving adequate levels of literacy (Commonwealth of Australia, 1997; House of Representatives Standing Committee on Employment

Education and Training, 1992) and that teachers were not being adequately trained to teach a full range of reading, writing and spelling skills in a systematic way. In 1997 the Education Ministers in the various states and territories agreed that one basic goal for primary education must be that every child leaving primary school should be numerate, and able to read, write *and spell* at an appropriate level (MCEETYA, 1997). The *National Literacy Plan* emerged, and the *Benchmarks for Literacy* were introduced in 2000, specifying clearly the standards to be expected of students in Year 3, Year 5 and Year 7 (Curriculum Corporation, 2000). The introduction of benchmarks saw spelling once again given the recognition it deserves, rather than being subsumed under the more general skill area of 'writing'.

The benchmarks, although not popular with some educators, have given a sense of direction for spelling instruction that was rather lacking in previous curriculum guidelines such as *English: A curriculum profile for Australian schools* (Curriculum Corporation, 1994). It was not until official documents began to specify in some detail the spelling skills and standards that students should display that spelling returned to the literacy agenda. To reinforce this, regular national testing of standards in spelling, grammar and punctuation for students in Years, 3, 5, 7 and 9 commenced in 2008.

In the United Kingdom, where whole language had also been the recommended approach to literacy teaching, concern was also being expressed about standards. The outcome was the formulation of the *National Literacy Strategy* that has had a direct and positive influence on classroom practice in recent years. The importance of explicit teaching of spelling in schools is strongly reinforced in the renewed *Primary Framework* (DES, 2006) in which spelling is identified as one of the 12 key strands of learning. There is an emphasis now on daily 'word study' and spelling within the 'literacy hour'; and the teaching of phonic knowledge (which underpins basic spelling ability) has become respectable again.

Reports in the United States of America, the United Kingdom and Australia calling for the use of research-based instructional methods for the teaching of basic academic skills have also had a potentially beneficial spin-off for strengthening instruction in spelling as well as reading and phonics (Ellis, 2005; House of Commons Education and Skills Committee, UK, 2005; National Reading Panel, US, 2000; Rose, 2005). These reports have reinforced the importance of direct teaching of essential literacy skills, particularly in the early stages of acquisition.

It would be folly, of course, to suppose that these documents have had any real impact yet on the thinking and practices of those teachers and teacher educators who remain ardent believers in 'whole language' and 'natural learning'. Nor can we assume that teacher educators have suddenly started including coverage of direct teaching approaches or instructional methods for spelling in their language arts methodology courses; that would be too much to hope for. The situation in pre-service teacher education is still much the same now as the one Bryan (2003, p. 14) remembers. She recalls, 'When I began teaching in 1991, spelling seemed to be a four-letter word. Spelling was an area almost untouched during my years [of teacher education] at university. I had no idea how to go about teaching students to learn to spell'.

Public interest in spelling was aroused again when *The Australian* carried a report indicating that 'Singapore kids spell better than Aussies' (Ferrari, 2006). It had been found that in a writing test conducted with large samples of students in both countries that about nine times more students in Singapore were able to spell less-common and irregular English words, compared to students in Australia. This is particularly impressive because about half the students in Singapore learn English as a second language. The conclusion was that Singaporean students' success was due to the use of direct and explicit instruction in schools. In a follow-up article in the *Weekend Australian*, Wheeldon (2006, p. 21) remarked: 'These results cannot be a surprise since we stopped serious teaching of spelling, grammar and sentence construction decades ago ... If you want good spelling and grammar, find someone over 55'. She commented also that 'a failure to teach spelling is a failure of duty of care'.

Current situation

Perhaps the most significant change since the 1990s can be seen in the fact that it is now respectable again to speak of *teaching* spelling, as opposed to arguing against such teaching. The growing body of research data clearly indicates that students become better spellers if learning is not left to chance (e.g., Canado, 2006; DuBois et al., 2007; Foorman et al., 2006; Strattman & Hodson, 2005). In particular, students with learning difficulties benefit greatly from direct instruction that helps them understand and apply the principles underpinning the construction of words in the English language (Frank, 2007; Joseph & Orlins, 2005; Vedora & Stromer, 2007). Of course, it is not a matter of *replacing* the use of students' own writing as a source of instruction, but rather of supplementing this contextualised teaching with a more structured approach to word study. As with all areas of literacy teaching, it is a matter of achieving the appropriate balance between whole-language student-centred principles and the direct teaching and practice that is necessary to establish essential skills (Egan & van Gorder, 1998).

Now that spelling is back on the agenda, most education authorities are providing guidelines for teachers (e.g., DECS, SA, 1997; DET, NSW, 1998; DE, Tas., 2007a) and for parents (e.g., Board of Studies, NSW, 2007). In most cases these guidelines are necessary in order to compensate for the fact that many teachers trained in the years between 1980 and 2000 received little or no guidance on how to teach spelling. Even today we cannot be sure that there has been much change in this respect within university departments of methodology and teaching practice. A single lecture or workshop session on the topic of spelling is totally inadequate for equipping teachers with the depth of required information and practical skills. Where teachers are gaining most professional benefit seems to be in schools where they have established a whole-school policy on the teaching of spelling and where teachers support one another in terms of acquiring new skills and understandings (Egan & van Gorder, 1998; Kervin & McKenzie, 2005).

It is not only in the area of policy and curriculum guidelines that growth occurred after the 1990s. The period between 1990 and 2007 saw a very significant increase in the number of well-designed research studies that explored aspects of spelling acquisition and the effectiveness of different methods of instruction (summarised in Schlagal, 2002; and Westwood, 2008). Several of these studies focused on spelling in alphabetic languages other than English (e.g., Cardoso-Martins et al., 2006; Rahbari et al., 2007) or on children learning English as a second or additional language (e.g., Lam & Westwood, 2006; Lipka & Siegel, 2007). Virtually all of these studies provide evidence that learning to spell is not a 'natural' process but rather a complex task involving many different perceptual, cognitive and linguistic skills. In the following chapters relevant information from some of this research is interpreted in practical terms.

Teachers' expertise

To be an effective teacher of spelling, one must have a genuine interest in words, their origin, meaning and construction, and must also have an understanding of the phonological, orthographic and morphographic principles and rules that govern English spelling. In particular, it is important that teachers also recognise and can articulate the various strategies that a speller can use when faced with spelling an unfamiliar word.

It cannot be denied that teachers' own knowledge of these concepts, principles and strategies, and of grammar as a whole, is often deficient (Hurry et al., 2005; Moats, 1994). For example, in the United States of America, Bos et al. (2001) discovered that many pre-service and serving teachers were ignorant of even basic principles of word structure such as the number of phonemes contained in a word like 'grass', or the second sound in the word 'queen'. A similar lack of knowledge, even related to syllables and basic phonics, was revealed in a study of pre-service teachers in Australia (Meehan & Hammond, 2006).

It is also reported that many teachers are also unaware of the developmental aspects of spelling and therefore do not really know what standard of accuracy they should be expecting from students at different ages (Johnson, 2001; Schlagal, 2001). As a result, even when they do feel that they should do something positive about spelling, they are likely to resort to the use of word lists and memorisation rather than teaching spelling as a thinking process (Fresch, 2007; Johnson, 2001). Although spelling lists exist that are developmentally appropriate and can be helpful in fostering spelling development, most lists are not of that type and their use is often counterproductive (Manning & Underbakke, 2005). More will be said about lists in a later chapter.

Finally, many teachers appear not to be fully aware of the various factors that can cause some students to have difficulties learning to spell. They are uncertain how to determine the instructional needs of weaker spellers and how to tailor their teaching to meet those needs.

Given these weaknesses in many teachers' content knowledge in relation to spelling, it is not surprising that spelling is not well taught, even though it is firmly back on the literacy agenda. The following chapters are intended to provide teachers with a better understanding of the main theoretical issues and practical approaches involved in teaching students to spell.

LINKS TO MORE ON KEY ISSUES IN SPELLING

- A conference paper containing much useful advice for approaching spelling as a whole-school policy issue, together with some useful practical advice for the classroom. Kervin, L. & McKenzie, K. (2005). Keeping the conversation going: Creating a whole school approach to spelling. *Conference proceedings: Pleasure, passion, provocation.* AATE/ALEA National Conference, 1–4 July 2005: Broadbeach, Qld. Retrieved December 16, 2007 from: http://alea.edu.au/site-content/Kervin_McKenzie.pdf
- Examples of spelling benchmarks for Year 3 and Year 5 online at QCA website for International Review of Curriculum and Assessment (INCA) at: http://www.inca.org.uk/australia-appendix-mainstream.html See also: http://www.dest.gov.au/sectors/school_education/policy_initiatives_reviews/key_issues/literacy_numeracy/national_literacy_and_numeracy_benchmarks.htm
- A discussion of standards in spelling is provided by Jennifer Chew (1999) online at: http://www.spellingsociety.org/journals/j25/chew.php
- A list of ten false assumptions about teaching spelling, compiled by Richard Gentry, provides an excellent discussion starter for school staff meetings and for teachers in the English Department. It can be found online at: http://jrichardgentry.com/text/ten_false_assumptions.pdf

two

The anatomy of spelling

> **KEY ISSUES**
>
> - Spelling is a complex skill and relies on a number of integrated perceptual, cognitive and linguistic sub-skills and processes.
> - Certain of these sub-skills and processes are more important than others at specific stages in development from beginning speller to proficient speller.
> - Reading experience is a necessary (but in itself insufficient) condition to foster accurate spelling.
> - Fluency in handwriting influences spelling accuracy to some degree.

Written language is acknowledged to be the most complex form of language that children must acquire. For example, Gregg and Mather (2002, p. 7) point out that, 'Writing competence is based on the successful orchestration of many abilities, including those needed for lower level transcription skills as well as those essential for higher level composing abilities'. Of these lower-level skills, spelling is one of the most important and, for some, the most difficult skill to acquire.

Competence in spelling requires, among other things, an understanding of the alphabetic principle, a thorough knowledge of letter-to-sound correspondences, phonological awareness that allows within-word sound units to be identified (syllables and phonemes), sensitivity to groups of letters that can and cannot occur together in English language (orthographic awareness), an understanding of the way in which the meaning of a word influences the spelling of that word, adequate visual perception, visual and motor memory, and the ability to write or use a keyboard (Chliounaki & Bryant, 2007; Treiman & Kessler, 2006). Senechal et al. (2006. p. 231) explain that, 'Learning to spell involves learning how to map speech sounds onto letters, learning how to apply the orthographic and grammatical rules of written language, and learning the exceptions to those rules'. They go on to stress that, 'Learning to spell involves more than mere memorisation of letter sequences because it also involves developing adaptive and efficient strategies'. Spelling is clearly not a 'natural' process and, for most individuals, learning to spell requires much conscious effort.

Sub-skills and processes in spelling

Understanding the nature of the sub-skills and processes involved in spelling helps teachers appreciate exactly how spelling skills are acquired and what forms of instruction may be necessary. Such understanding can also help teachers identify the specific difficulties a student may have with spelling.

Visual perception and visual memory

Becoming a good speller involves, among other things, the ability to internalise and remember the visual characteristics of words. Visual memory is needed not only in the initial stages of learning a new word but also in the final stages when checking and proofreading one's attempts at spelling that word. The most common way of checking spelling and detecting errors is to look carefully at the written word and ask oneself, 'Does this word look right?' Writers will sometimes stop while writing simply because a word they have written doesn't 'look right' on the page, and they may decide to refer to a dictionary or spell-checker.

Andrews and Scarratt (1996) observed that skilled spelling reflects highly effective lexical storage and retrieval processes that are dependent on memory. Our 'lexical memory' contains images of many words and (even more importantly) *parts of words* that can be recalled automatically when needed. These images of spelling patterns are acquired partly as the result of exposure to the words during reading, but even more through frequently writing those words (Noell et al., 2006).

For many years, learning to spell was regarded as predominantly a visual and visual-motor (writing) process (e.g., Peters, 1970; 1974; 1985). It was often argued that since the English language contains a proportion of words that do not adhere to phonic principles, it was therefore necessary to remember words as letter patterns rather than attempting to spell them by reference to their phonemes. More recently, it has been acknowledged that spelling relies more on phonological information, particularly in the beginning stages, than it does on visual information; and 'sounding out' a word is often an effective strategy.

It may be that learners are more dependent on visual processing and visual memory strategies at certain stages on the way to becoming proficient spellers. The increasing ability to store a bank of high-frequency words in visual memory and to recognise commonly occurring orthographic units are the two main characteristics of what is called the 'transitional stage' of spelling development (see Chapter 3). As students move out of the phonetic stage of spelling, they begin to rely much more on the visual characteristics of a word, particularly for proofreading and checking purposes, and very much less on a simple translation from sound to symbol.

Of course, some English words do not conform at all to phonic principles (e.g. *ask, said, choir*) and have to be mastered by visual methods of learning, backed up by repeated writing to establish the irregular spelling pattern in memory. This is sometimes referred to as the 'whole word' spelling strategy.

Phonological awareness

It has been known for more than 20 years that the ability to detect separate speech sounds (phonemes) within spoken words and to manipulate these sounds mentally underpins students' successful entry into reading and writing (Bryant & Bradley, 1983; Hempenstall, 2002; Williams, 1986). Understanding the alphabetic principle requires a child to recognise that each spoken word contains a sequence of separate sounds (Eldredge, 2005). Without this phonological ability, it is impossible for a child to learn to decode and encode words using phonic principles. This ability, generally referred to as *phonological awareness* or *phonemic awareness*, is important both for reading and for spelling. It is often reported that phonological skills in young children are the best single predictors of their later reading and spelling ability (Critten et al., 2007; Plaza & Cohen, 2007; Rahbari et al., 2007; Strattman & Hodson, 2005).

Phonological awareness is important not only in learning to read and write in English but in other languages too (e.g., Hilte et al., 2005; Ho & Bryant, 1997; Lipka & Siegel, 2007; Rahbari et al., 2007). Even learning to read in languages that are not based on an alphabetic code (e.g. Chinese) seem to require that the learner understands how spoken words can be analysed or sub-divided (Ho et al., 2002).

Phonological awareness manifests itself in seven main skills. The skills are those that are deliberately trained in programs designed to develop phonological abilities in young children and in children with reading or spelling difficulties (e.g., Blachman et al., 2000; Moore, et al., 2005). The skills comprise:

- *Auditory discrimination:* This is the basic ability to detect similarities and differences among speech sounds; for example, to know that the /f/ sound and the /th/ sound are different, as in *finger* and *thumb*; or that *church* and *children* both begin with the same /ch/ sound. In addition to the primary function of identifying and differentiating sounds in words, the ability to pronounce words accurately is also dependent on auditory discrimination. Correct pronunciation is important for accurate spelling.
- *Auditory analysis (or segmentation):* This is the ability to analyse spoken sentences mentally into words, words into syllables and syllables into separate sounds. Awareness of syllables and syllable sub-units (*onset* and *rime*) tends to develop before the ability to identify each separate phoneme in a word. The terms *onset* and *rime* refer to the two units that are created when any single-syllable word is sub-divided (e.g. *truck* = /tr/ + /uck/; *home* = /h/ + /ome/.
- *Sound blending (or phoneme blending):* This is the ability mentally and vocally to combine speech sounds into syllables and syllables into words. It is a vital skill for both decoding in reading and encoding when spelling.
- *Rhyming:* This is the ability to detect words that rhyme and to produce rhyming words. Rhyming is the basis upon which children begin to understand that words sharing a common sound pattern probably share some common sequences of letters (e.g. *bet, get, jet, let, met, net*). This is the first stage in developing an awareness of orthographic units. More will be said of this later.
- *Alliteration:* This is recognising when a series of words contain a common initial sound (e.g. 'Green grasshoppers are greedy').

- *Isolation:* This is the ability to identify not only the initial sound in a word but also final and medial sounds. For example, knowing that *doll* begins with the /d/ sound, ends with the /ll/ sound, and has /o/ in the middle.
- *Exchanging:* The mental ability to move sounds into different positions in a word (*bat* becomes *tab*; *cheat* becomes *teach*) or substitute a new sound for another sound to produce a new word: (*met* becomes *pet*; *lost* becomes *cost*).

Auditory discrimination, auditory analysis and sound blending are regarded as the key aspects of phonological awareness, and they are essential for the development of spelling skills. According to Weeks et al. (2002), the act of spelling is to a large degree a phonological translation task. A significant lack of phonological awareness – for example, as is the case with students who are deaf – has a serious impact on their spelling ability (Wakefield, 2006). Many other students with spelling difficulties, particularly those with dyslexia, also show poorly developed phonological analysis skills (Vukovic & Siegel, 2006). Accurate identification of the sounds at the ends of words appears to be particularly difficult for some dyslexic students. They are reported to have major problems identifying endings such as *–ed, –ent, –er, –ly, –ally, –ous, –ent* (Moats, 1995).

As indicated above, in the earliest stages of learning to spell, children rely very heavily on knowledge of letter-to-sound correspondences. Their 'invented' spellings reveal the extent to which they are beginning to identify sounds within words and their ability to match these sounds with letters (Kolodziej & Columba, 2005). More will be said about the main stages involved in acquiring spelling proficiency.

Given that there are 44 speech sounds in English, but only 26 letters available to represent them, it is clear that a simple phonetic approach to spelling has some limitations. Although phonological awareness and phonic knowledge help greatly with the spelling of very many words, it is clear that other sources of information are also needed at times to guide the production of correct spellings. These other sources include orthographic awareness and a grasp of morphemic principles. Notenboom and Reitsma (2003, p. 1039) state:

> Phoneme awareness and knowledge of grapheme–phoneme correspondences are critical in the early stages of learning to spell. Later, grammatical and morphological knowledge, analogies with words in lexical memory,

and the knowledge of orthographic rules and conventions become important as well.

Orthographic awareness

As stated above, accurate spelling of words in English is greatly facilitated when an individual moves beyond knowing the single letter-to-sound correspondences and reaches the stage of mastering groups of letters that occur together and result in larger pronounceable units. For example, in the word *tight*, the individual sounds represented by the letters 'i', 'g', 'h' and 't' do not in any way assist with the decoding or encoding of *tight*. But knowing that the rime /ight/ can be represented by the orthographic units 'ight' or 'ite' make it much more likely that the speller will select the correct letters or will write a plausible phonetic alternative. At least 80 per cent of English words can be spelled according to phonic principles if we attend to *groups of letters* representing pronounceable parts of words, such as *–tion* or *pre–* or *–ought* (orthographic units) rather than to single letter-to-sound correspondences (Schlagal, 2001). If spelling is based on orthographic units, only some 3 per cent of words remain true spelling demons.

Steffler (2001) observes that as children emerge from the simplest level of phonetic spelling they begin to recognise common features in words and to map them to particular orthographic patterns. Orthographic knowledge is thus acquired as children gain experience with reading and writing and become more aware of the kinds of common letter sequences that occur together within the language. Some researchers view this process of noting the frequency and probability that certain letters can occur together as a form of 'statistical' learning that helps spellers predict correct letter sequences (Treiman & Kessler, 2006). Acquiring orthographic awareness is also facilitated by specific training and practice activities, such as studying word families and using word sorts (see Chapter 5).

Developing orthographic awareness marks a major advance towards becoming a proficient speller. Notenboom and Reitsma (2003) suggest that learning to spell in the primary school years mainly consists of learning to acquire and apply orthographic knowledge. They believe that the transition from alphabetic (phonic) spelling to use of the more effective orthographic strategy usually begins in Grade 1 for normally developing children. Spelling skills then begin to develop rapidly as most children become more able to map orthographic units, rather than single letters, to the pronunciation of a word (Cardoso-Martins et al., 2006).

It is clear that an important goal in any effective spelling program is helping students take advantage of the regularities and patterns underlying English spelling. As children become increasingly aware of spelling patterns and their applications, they can better predict the structure of unknown words. They can also make greater use of the strategy of spelling by analogy (that is, using the spelling of a known word to help with the spelling of an unfamiliar word). Development in this direction is helped by teaching children to think also in terms of *morphemes* when spelling more complex words.

Morphological awareness

Morphemes are the smallest units of meaning that exist in a language. A *morphograph* is the written form of a morpheme. An awareness of morphemes, and how they combine in English spelling, is helpful for all spellers.

A single word may represent one morpheme, for example *sad* or *happy*. By adding other morphemes to *sad* and *happy* we can make *sadness*, *sadly*, *happiness* (all containing two morphemes) and *unhappiness* (containing three morphemes). Similarly, the verb *play* represents one morpheme, but to change it to *playing* or *played* we add another morpheme. Morphemes are represented by base words, prefixes and suffixes, and in changes that signal variations in verb tense, possession, or plurality. Often the adding of a morpheme must obey certain rules (for example the changing of 'y' to 'i' in *happiness*, as above, or sometimes doubling a letter as in the change from *travel* to *travelling*).

Steffler (2001) suggests that spelling development normally progresses from a phonological level to a higher-order *morphological* level, and then to a level where both these aspects are taken into account. Knowledge of morphological principles can enhance spelling ability (e.g., Nunes et al., 2003). When students become familiar with meaningful units such as prefixes and suffixes, as well as root or base words, their grasp of word structure expands. Research in recent years has increasingly placed importance on understanding and using morphological information and principles to improve spelling (e.g., Kemp, 2006; Nunes et al., 1997; Verhoeven & Carlisle, 2006). Templeton (2004, p. 48) remarks:

> [T]eachers must step away from the expectation that English spelling is highly irregular because it doesn't represent sounds in a consistent manner. English is more consistent in representing sound than is often realized, but it also represents meaning quite consistently through its consistent spelling of prefixes, suffixes and most base words and Latin and Greek root words.

While it is true that some children begin to discover morphological principles for themselves through their experiences with reading and writing (Chliounaki & Bryant, 2007; Kemp, 2006), it is equally true that most children need to be taught this information in order to make use of it. Teaching children about morphemes has been shown to have a beneficial effect on their spelling ability (e.g., Nunes et al., 2003). Unfortunately, it seems that many teachers do not explicitly teach children anything at all about morphemes and word structure. In a study by Hurry et al. (2005) only 3 out of 17 teachers could even define a morpheme. The relative lack of instruction in morphological principles represents a significant gap between what research has shown to be important and what teachers actually do in the classroom.

Spelling programs do exist that are based on morphological principles (e.g. *Spelling through Morphographs* and *Spelling Mastery 2007* from Science Research Associates) but these are not widely used in Australian or British classrooms (see the Link box at the end of the chapter).

The reading–spelling connection

Do we learn to spell mainly from our experiences with reading? Spelling ability was once considered merely a by-product of reading experience. It was believed that as children build a memory bank of words known by sight, they will simultaneously be able to write and spell those words. Wilde (2004) remarks that reading is the single most important factor in spelling development because children need to engage with words in print, particularly words that are not phonetically regular. Frequent reading is the chief means by which children are exposed to words and thus become familiar with orthographic units. It is certainly an attractive proposition to think that we learn the correct spellings of words from seeing them frequently in print. But is it true?

Some experts in literacy teaching maintain that there is indeed a close relationship between reading and spelling, and that learning about spelling enhances reading ability, and *vice versa* (e.g., Graham et al., 2002; Noell et al., 2006; Santoro et al., 2006; Schlagal, 2001). Learning to apply phonic skills for reading purposes provides at the same time a very necessary skill required for spelling. In reverse, there is evidence to suggest that instruction in spelling has a beneficial impact on children's reading in the early years of schooling (Berninger et al., 1998; Gentry, 2004). Reading also represents one way in which children begin to discover information about morphemes, which in turn supports spelling development (Nunes et al., 2006).

However, the consensus among researchers now is that spelling and reading are not simply the same process employed in reverse, and that the influence of reading on spelling development is actually less than one might imagine (e.g., Bradley, 1983; Clarke-Klein, 1994; Ehri, 1997; Peters, 1974). One sometimes finds an individual who is a good reader but a very poor speller; so good reading ability is obviously no guarantee that good spelling ability will follow. Simply seeing words through reading text does not teach spelling, and children do not automatically become good spellers simply by engaging in reading. Perhaps this is because reading (decoding) is a different and separate process from spelling (encoding), although drawing on some of the same underlying knowledge and skills. Reading is relatively more adaptable than spelling because one uses additional contextual clues to aid word recognition. Indeed, with the support of context of a sentence, readers often pay minimal attention to separate letters and letter groups, instead working almost entirely from meaning, not from decoding. Spelling, on the other hand, requires accurate retrieval and reproduction of sequences of letters that cannot be guided at all from context. According to Mastropieri and Scruggs (2002), spelling is a more difficult activity than reading because it requires *production* of a correct sequence of letters. Reading, on the other hand, requires *recognition* of a set of symbols already displayed on the page. Recognition is usually an easier memory process than recall and production. For most weak spellers, recalling the correct sequence of letters is the major obstacle.

There are individual differences among spellers as to how much benefit for spelling they gain from reading. Weaker readers are reported to be the least likely to improve simply by doing more reading (Graham, 2000). In general, the conclusion must be that individuals learn words much less efficiently from simply reading them compared with other types of more active spelling practice with corrective feedback (Holmes & Davis, 2002). Reading words is a necessary but insufficient condition to ensure that children acquire an understanding of the principles underpinning spelling patterns. Explicit instruction, particularly in word study and learning strategies for spelling, is likely to achieve very much more in helping students become better spellers. Practical suggestions for such teaching are provided in later chapters.

The spelling–handwriting connection

According to Nichols (1985), accurate spelling is remembered best in the hand. In other words, we subconsciously recall and reproduce the swift movements of pen, pencil or keyboard that led to the correct sequence of letters on previous occasions. The rapid speed and automaticity with which a competent speller writes known words strongly supports the view that motor memory is involved in spelling, at least to some extent. The action of writing or typing a word frequently is one of the ways of establishing our memory bank of images of orthographic units (DE, Tas., 2007b). Richards (1999, p. 66) attributes problems in both handwriting and spelling to an underlying weakness in 'sequential motor memory'.

Milone et al. (1983) conducted an investigation into the relationship between handwriting and spelling. They found a fairly strong association between the two. Similarly, as a result of her detailed studies in the United Kingdom, Margaret Peters (1985) regarded accurate spelling as being quite closely connected with swift and fluent handwriting. Roaf (1998), studying the handwriting of secondary school students in the United Kingdom, found that slow writers exhibited problems with letter formation, discrimination between upper and lower case letters, and accuracy in spelling.

It cannot be inferred, of course, that good handwriting *per se* causes good spelling, but it is clear that uncertain letter formation and slow writing habits inhibit easy development of automaticity in spelling (Delattre et al., 2006). It has even been suggested that children's spelling development is aided by teaching them a simple style of joined handwriting in the early school years, rather than first teaching them to print each separate letter and only later introducing joined style (Cripps, 1990). Moseley (1997) queries this practice, however, indicating that there is little evidence to support it.

The practical implications from the handwriting–spelling connection are that, firstly teachers in the early school years do need to teach children an easy style of writing that can be mastered and executed without requiring major cognitive effort (Spear-Swerling, 2006). Children are then in the best position to focus their attention on spelling patterns. Secondly, if a child has a problem with handwriting, every effort should be made to help him or her acquire a more effective and fluent style. Thirdly, it must be acknowledged that writing words neatly and fluently many times can, *in certain circumstances*, be an effective teaching and remedial approach. The circumstances under which it is an effective method are discussed in Chapter 6.

LINKS TO MORE ON SPELLING SKILLS AND PROCESSES

- A comprehensive list of pertinent references covering reading and spelling sub-skills can be found at the Southwest Educational Development Laboratory (SEDL) at: http://www.sedl.org/reading/framework/references.html#Bruck
- *Teaching phonics in the National Literacy Strategy* (United Kingdom). Available online at: http://www.standards.dfes.gov.uk/pdf/literacy/nls_phonics.pdf
- For information on the programs *Spelling through Morphographs* and *Spelling Mastery 2007*, see: http://www.sraonline.com/download/SpellingMastery/MoreInfo/MC1602%20SpellingBroch_FA4_snglpg.pdf
- Useful material on the importance of encouraging children's awareness and understanding of morphemes in relation to spelling can be found at the Teaching and Learning Program website at: http://www.tlrp.org/pub/documents/no14_nunes.pdf
- A paper by Milone et al., discussing the link between handwriting and spelling can be located online at: http://www.spellingsociety.org/bulletins/b83/summer/handwriting.php
- Additional advice on handwriting is provided in Spear-Swerling, L. (2006) *The importance of teaching handwriting* at the LD Online website: http://www.ldonline.org/spearswerling/10521

three

Developmental and strategic aspects of spelling

KEY ISSUES

- The acquisition of spelling ability follows a developmental sequence reflecting an individual's increasing awareness of linguistic features.
- Spelling development also requires an individual to learn to apply increasingly effective strategies for learning new words and to check what is written.
- There is great variation among students in their discovery and use of spelling strategies.
- Teaching weaker spellers to apply more effective strategies for learning, checking and self-correcting words is a powerful way of addressing their instructional needs.

Since the pioneering work of Read (1971), Henderson and Beers (1980), and Ehri and Wilce (1985), an individual's acquisition of spelling knowledge has been recognised as a developmental process. Studies have suggested that children's spelling ability typically passes through a series of stages, each stage reflecting an advance in knowledge about phonemes, letters and letter-strings, and units of meaning within words. The stages also reflect the degree to which children have acquired effective strategies for analysing, checking and self-correcting words.

Children progress through the stages at different rates and with differing degrees of success. Their rates of progress and degrees of success are influenced not only by innate features (e.g. intelligence, reading ability, perceptual skills and memory) but also by the quality of the instruction they have received. Some children with a natural aptitude for spelling will progress quite rapidly, with little or no explicit teaching (Manning & Underbakke, 2005). Others will make much greater progress if explicitly taught the knowledge, skills and strategies needed to take them from one stage to the next. If teachers are aware of the stages in spelling development already reached by their students, they are better able (in theory anyway) to adapt their instruction to an appropriate level and to focus on developmentally appropriate words and strategies.

Stages in spelling development

Some researchers have identified four stages, others as many as seven. The actual terms that have been used to label the various stages of development differ from researcher to researcher, but listed below are the most common.

Stage 1: Pre-phonemic

At this stage, children try to imitate writing by copying down or inventing random strings of letters. The letters have no relationship at all to speech sounds and cannot be decoded into real words. Capital letters are used more frequently than lower case letters; and often the most commonly used letters are those found within the child's own name (Treiman et al., 2001).

Stage 2: Early phonetic

Gradually, children begin to make the connection that letters are meant to represent sounds. They then use incidentally acquired knowledge of letter names and sounds in an attempt to write words (e.g. *CN u rd?* = Can you read?; *lefNt* = elephant; *erpln* = aeroplane; *rsk* = ask). Consonants are used much more consistently than vowels. Some researchers suggest that at this stage a single letter is often used to represent a whole syllable because the child has yet to discover that syllables contain other sounds (Cardoso-Martins et al., 2006).

This early phonetic stage heralds the start of children's 'invented' spelling. Inventing words will continue to be used as their main strategy until they acquire other methods of determining more accurate spellings of the words they wish to write. Invented spellings provide the teacher with a clear indication of a child's awareness of the internal sound structure of spoken words and how these units can be represented with letters.

Stage 3: Phonetic

While most researchers refer to this as the *phonetic stage*, there are actually several sub-stages within it. In the beginning children are simply extending their experience from the pre-phonetic stage and making more accurate use of sound–symbol relationships. Children will attempt to spell difficult words, some of which result in good approximations, others less so. Most irregular words are written as if they are phonetically regular (e.g. *sed = said*; *becos = because*; *wos = was*).

Children moving through this stage become better able to identify sounds within words. In the intermediate stage they may still have difficulty in discriminating certain sounds accurately enough to match them with the appropriate letter or letter cluster. This difficulty is reflected in some of the words they write (e.g. *sbin = spin*; *sdop = stop*; *druck = truck*; *grive = drive*; *chrane = train*; *sboon = spoon*) (Hannam et al., 2007). They may also have difficulty attending to certain sounds within a word (e.g. they may write *bow* for *blow*; *srong* for *strong*; *chch* for *church*). At this stage they are not yet experienced enough to use visual checking to determine whether the word looks correct.

Towards the end of the phonetic stage, a few common orthographic units are remembered and reproduced easily and accurately (e.g. *un–*, *–ing*, *–ed*). A few common vowel digraphs also become known (e.g. *–ee–*, *–oo–*).

It should be noted that many older children with poor spelling skills have reached this phonetic stage in their development but have not progressed beyond it. They have remained at what Templeton (2003) refers to as a 'phonocentric' stage in which they rely too much on phonic cues alone. They need to be taught to use strategies such as visual imagery and spelling by analogy.

Stage 4: Transitional

At this stage there is evidence that children have acquired a much more sophisticated understanding of word structure. They are becoming increasingly confident in using commonly occurring orthographic units such as *–ough*, *–ious*, *–ai–*, *–aw–* to represent sounds within words. They are also making greater use of spelling by analogy; that is, using their knowledge of a known word to guide their spelling of a similar word.

Children at this stage are now relying much more on visual checking strategies rather than phonetic cues alone to determine the accuracy of what they have written. They are also becoming more aware of the way in which meaning helps to indicate the probable spelling of a given word. In other words, morphological information, and any rules that apply, are helping with the spelling of complex words (e.g. *penalty – penalties*, but *monkey – monkeys*).

Stage 5: Independence

At this stage children have almost perfect mastery of even the most complex grapho-phonic principles. Occasionally, a word will still give them some difficulty; but they will have available for use a very wide range of strategies for checking and self-correcting words. Proofreading skills are used with increasing proficiency but children at the independence stage will still make some careless errors and fail to detect them when proofreading their work.

Most students who are progressing normally and engaging in a great deal of writing have stored a considerable mental lexicon of correct word images. They can write almost all common words with a high degree of automaticity, and they have an increasing pool of knowledge of orthographic units from which to draw when attempting to spell unfamiliar words. Students who engage in a great deal of reading are adding significantly to this bank of word images through increased exposure to print; and conversely, students who read very little are likely to remain at the phonetic stage when spelling.

Beyond stage theory

While it is obvious that spelling ability does develop over time, as described above, some experts have expressed dissatisfaction that developmental stage theory fails to take account of the variation that exists among spellers of the same age in the way that they attempt to tackle the writing of unfamiliar words. Children's thinking and responses are highly variable when faced with particular words. Stage theory seems to imply that at particular ages and stages, spellers will all be using a similar approach – be it phonetic, orthographic or morphographic – but the reality is that when one examines the spelling of a group of students of a given age, the strategies said to be typical of that stage are not so distinct (Notenboom & Reitsma, 2003). Individual spellers, even from the earliest stages, may reveal that they have several different ways of attempting to spell words. These different strategies co-exist over prolonged periods, some being relatively important for a time only to give way later to others, while not being totally abandoned. And groups of children of a certain age may exhibit many different spelling strategies. More recent theories of spelling development have attempted to account for these variations (e.g., Rittle-Johnson & Siegler, 1999).

Overlapping waves theory is one recent perspective that goes beyond simple stage theory. Based on the work of Siegler (1996; 2000) who first applied it to strategies children use for simple arithmetic, overlapping wave theory suggests that the frequency of use of different strategies children possess or acquire rises and falls over a period of time, with a gradual increase in efficiency and sophistication. The concept can be visualised most clearly as a sequence of overlapping bell curves forming a wave-like progression from left to right. Each curve depicts the rise and fall in frequency of using a particular strategy or returning to use an earlier strategy. Rather than a neat linear progression from naivety to sophistication, children's learning appears to occur in waves (Bower, 2001). The theory specifies that learning occurs along four dimensions (a) more frequent use of the more effective ways of thinking; (b) increasingly adaptive choices among the available strategies; (c) increasing efficiency in executing the alternative strategies; and (d) acquisition of new ways of thinking.

Strategies for spelling

A strategy can be defined as a mental plan of action that enables an individual to approach a particular task in a systematic manner. Spelling a word is one such task; competent spellers possess a repertoire of effective spelling strategies and can apply them appropriately as needed.

Kervin and McKenzie (2005) point out that spelling should be regarded as a thinking process involving a strategic approach, not a rote-learning task. It is important that teachers help students add to their existing repertoire of spelling and proofreading strategies. An aim of effective teaching of spelling is to help students become more strategic in their approach. O'Sullivan (2000) reported that the most effective teachers of spelling helped students develop a variety of spelling strategies and drew their attention to common spelling patterns through analogy with other known words. New strategies may relate to deliberate and more effective use of phonological features of words (including those revealed in clear pronunciation), better use of visual characteristics of words and attention to morphological features. They may also involve effective strategies for learning and memorising words, such as enhancing visual imagery, repeated writing of a word, comparing incorrect with correct versions of a word and developing mnemonics to aid later recall. The teaching of some of these approaches will be discussed further in Chapter 5 and Chapter 6.

As indicated above, even young children display some degree of strategic behaviour when attempting to write a word correctly; often they have more than one strategy that they call upon as appropriate (Harrison, 2005; Senechal et al., 2006). In the study of children's spelling conducted by Rittle-Johnson and Siegler (1999), students were assessed in Grade 1 and again in Grade 2. The study employed a method that combined direct observation of performance with asking each child to explain the strategy he or she used to spell particular words. The study was conducted to determine whether the 'overlapping waves theory' discovered in relation to basic arithmetic also applied to spelling. To some extent, the theory was supported by the findings. Results indicated that every student used more than one strategy (the range being from two to five different strategies) and that there was flexibility in their selection. The strategies identified were classified as:

- *Retrieval from memory:* The word was correctly recalled immediately.
- *Sounding out:* The word was attempted after working out the phonemes and applying phonic knowledge.
- *Part retrieve/part sound out:* When only part of a word could be retrieved from memory, the remaining part was sounded out.
- *Analogy:* Recalling the spelling of a word that was similar to the target word.
- *Relying on rules:* Remembering, for example, to drop the final 'e' from *take* when spelling *taking*.
- *Visual checking:* Making sure that when a word was written it appeared to be correct (and then sometimes self-correcting, if necessary).

The most commonly used strategies at both age levels were retrieval and sounding out. Part retrieve/part sounding out, analogy, relying on rules and visual checking all increased in frequency in Grade 2. Rule use and visual checking were only ever used in conjunction with one of the other strategies.

An earlier study by Ormrod and Jenkins (1989) used students from three different age groups: Grades 3/4, Grades 7/8, and an undergraduate group. They used the method of requiring subjects to 'think aloud' as they studied ten unknown words. Seven categories of strategy were identified:

- *Pronunciation:* Saying the word aloud in a normal manner.
- *Over-enunciation (sometimes called spelling pronunciation):* Deliberately stressing the sound units within the word with exaggerated expression (e.g. *Wed – NES – day*; *Feb – RU – ary*).
- *Visual imagery:* Remembering a word as a letter sequence or pattern.
- *Rehearsal of letters:* Repeating aloud the names of the letters in sequence.
- *Word analysis:* Paying attention to roots, prefixes and suffixes; using analogy with other known words.
- *Spelling rules:* Remembering and applying appropriate rules.
- *Miscellaneous:* Other non-strategic methods.

The most common strategies were pronunciation and letter rehearsal; but interestingly, these strategies were not positively correlated with later test scores. Letter rehearsal was used mainly by younger students and was negatively associated with spelling. Only the undergrads used over-enunciation (spelling pronunciation) and for them it was significantly correlated (0.51) with test scores.

Holmes and Malone (2004) also used the self-report and think aloud method to target the spelling strategies used by adults as they attempted to re-learn previously misspelled words. They discovered that five different strategies were available for use, namely (in order of frequency):

- letter rehearsal
- over-enunciation
- comparing incorrect with correct spelling
- morphological analysis
- visualisation.

The poorer spellers in the sample used much less over-enunciation, comparison and morphological analysis. Hilte et al. (2005) suggest that over-enunciation may be of no help to weaker spellers who tend to be lacking in phonological awareness. However, the strategies of comparing an incorrect spelling with a correct model, and making better use of morphemes would seem to be strategies that have simply not been taught to these students, and could easily be the focus of strategy training.

An Australian study of students in Year 5 identified as many as 19 possible strategies that spellers might use (Ralston & Robinson, 1997). These researchers concluded that spelling accuracy is enhanced when several strategies for generating and checking words are applied in combination, a view shared by Dahl et al. (2003). The writers comment that if students were to be taught explicitly to use a greater variety of spelling strategies, they might use them more effectively and selectively when they write.

The importance of teaching effective strategies for spelling

While it is true that students do devise their own strategies for learning words and for attempting to write unfamiliar words, their strategies are not always the most effective. There can be no doubt that improvement in spelling can be achieved if students are taught more about how to learn words and how to check the spelling of the words they have attempted. Many studies have indicated that to eradicate the inefficient rote memorisation method often adopted by students, it is important to teach them more effective spelling strategies (e.g., Chandler, 2000; Dahl et al., 2003; Ralston & Robinson, 1997; Wheatley, 2005).

There are many strategies that can be taught. Senechal et al. (2006) suggest that they can be broadly categorised as phonological, orthographic, morphographic and mnemonic. Within the research literature, the most frequently cited strategies falling into these various categories include the following examples.

Spell it as it sounds

This strategy is simply building on children's natural inclination to invent the spelling of a word based on the syllables and sounds they can hear within the spoken word. Dahl and her associates (2003) suggested that this is an important early strategy that helps students become more proficient within the 'phonetic' stage of spelling development.

For older students, this strategy has been applied in an approach called *Fonetik Spelling* (Jackson, 1994; Jackson et al., 2003). The approach is described fully in Chapter 6.

Look-say-cover-write-check

This strategy encourages accurate visual imagery and has been popular for many years. It is very effective for learning words that contain irregular letter-to-sound correspondences (e.g. *any, choir, juice*). The strategy has been well researched (e.g., Bryan, 2003; Cates et al., 2007; Keller, 2002; Nies & Belfiore, 2006). These writers conclude that the strategy is effective for improving recall of spelling patterns, and that the self-checking and self-correction aspects of the method strengthen students' autonomy in spelling. Kelly (2006) warns, however, that because the look-say-cover-write-check strategy relies mainly on visual memory of individual words, it needs to be supplemented by direct teaching of word analysis skills. Students must also have access to other more analytical ways of learning words.

One version of the approach involves presenting a word on a card to the learner. The learner is told:

- Use your eyes like a camera. Take a mental picture of this word.
- Close your eyes and imagine you can still see the word.
- Trace the letters in the air with your eyes closed.
- What colour are the letters in your mind?
- OK. Now imagine the letters have changed colour. What colour are they now?
- Open your eyes and write the word on your paper.
- Now check your spelling with the word on the card.

Berninger et al. (1995) taught specific spelling strategies to students with spelling problems at the end of Grade 3 as part of a general intervention to improve their writing skills. In particular, they taught a visual imagery strategy for spelling. They also taught strategies for analysing words into syllables. The benefits of the training were still evident six months later.

The students were taught the following steps:

- Look at the word.
- Close your eyes and imagine you can see the word as you say it.
- Name the letters from left to right.

- Open your eyes and write the word.
- Check against the model.
- Repeat if necessary until the word can be recalled easily.

Self-directing strategy

It is helpful to teach all students some form of self-regulatory strategy to use when learning new words or when checking spelling at the proofreading stage of writing (Lam & Westwood, 2006). A typical self-help strategy involves a student in:

- saying the target word
- repeating the word slowly
- counting the syllables
- attempting to write the syllables in sequence, matching letters and letter-groups to sounds
- checking the visual appearance of the word while again saying the word slowly in segments
- repeating the process if necessary until satisfied
- checking with other sources if still not satisfied (dictionary, spell-checker, another student or adult).

Spelling by analogy

Knowing the correct spelling of the one word can facilitate the spelling of other words that are related by sound or visual patterns. For example, knowing how to spell *take* facilitates the spelling of words such as *make, lake, break, baker* and *bakery*. Kirkbride and Wright (2002) found that children's spelling ability is enhanced if they are taught explicitly how to make use of this type of analogical approach. Use of analogy is a strategy that should be covered thoroughly in any word study sessions (see Chapter 5). The effective use of *word families* is one way of helping children notice and remember common elements contained within and across words.

Using knowledge of morphemes

Morphological knowledge is important within the English spelling system because many words share particular orthographic units that signal a meaning (Kelman & Apel, 2004; Senechal et al., 2006). Some experts argue that the most efficient way to store spelling patterns in long-term memory may be by their morphemes rather than by their whole-word forms because morphemic units can be generalised most easily to other spelling situations (Elbro & Arnbak, 1996; Teaching & Learning Research Project, 2006). As explained in Chapter 2, morphological knowledge refers to awareness of the functions of morphemes as the smallest units of language that can carry meaning (e.g. base words, prefixes, suffixes). Morphological knowledge helps spellers work out relationships between base words (e.g. *hunt, cover, talk, prosper*) and related inflected or derived words (e.g. *hunting, hunter, hunted; covered, recover, recovery, discover; talking, talkative; prosperous, prosperity*). At a simple level, a knowledge of morphemes includes such understandings as adding 's' to form many plural nouns, adding 'ed' to many past tense verbs, or 'ing' to present tense, and later knowing common prefixes and suffixes, such as *dis–, un–, anti–, pre–, –ness, –ity, –al, –ious*.

Deacon and Bryant (2006) suggest that many students in middle primary years intuitively use information about base words and the units of meaning we add to them. However, using morphological knowledge is a more advanced and cognitively demanding type of strategy compared to the four described above, and therefore usually needs to be taught explicitly.

Darch et al. (2000) suggest that many students with learning difficulties benefit greatly from explicit instruction that helps them understand morphemic principles. Unfortunately, the Teaching and Learning Research Project (2006) discovered that teachers themselves are rarely aware of the importance of teaching basic morphology, and often lack any depth of understanding in that domain.

Over-enunciation

Studies have suggested that exaggerating the pronunciation of tricky words by breaking them into pronounceable units and stressing the sounds that may be overlooked when writing does make the task of spelling such words more manageable (e.g. *Wed – NES – day; re – MEM – ber; re – HEAR – sal*) (Hilte & Reitsma, 2006). The strategy is also referred to as *spelling pronunciation*. It appears to be a fairly advanced self-help strategy, employed mainly by older spellers. It is, however, a strategy that is reasonably easy to teach and can be modelled quite clearly by teachers, for example, when giving dictation or presenting words in spelling tests.

Recitation (letter rehearsal)

This strategy is one that many individuals adopt spontaneously. It involves simply repeating aloud several times the sequence of sounds (or more commonly, the names) of the letters in the word and then saying the word. For example, *g – r – e – e – n, green*; *g– r – e – e – n, green*, etc. While it is popular with many spellers in both primary and secondary school, it has not been found to be very effective in terms of long-term recall of the spelling of the recited words (Ormrod & Jenkins, 1989).

A more formalised version of this strategy is represented in the remedial procedure known as *simultaneous oral spelling* (SOS), described fully in Chapter 6. Studies have given support to the value of SOS for the learning of irregular words, where a phonological strategy is ineffective (e.g., Bryant & Bradley, 1985; Weeks et al., 2002).

Mnemonics

A mnemonic is any verbal device that is designed to aid memory. Although mnemonics are often referred to as helpful for spelling, they are actually of fairly limited value and highly specific in application. Mnemonics are probably most helpful for the individual who knows that the spelling of one particular word always gives trouble. Examples of mnemonics include: 'Remember, the princiPAL is your pal' (to help differentiate the spelling of *principle* and *principal*). 'The cAR is stationARy' (to differentiate between *stationery* and *stationary*). 'NeCeSSary has 1 collar and 2 sleeves'. 'To spell *believe*, remember it has a LIE in it' (to avoid the 'ie' or 'ei' confusion). Some simple spelling rules can also be regarded as mnemonics; for example, 'I before E, except after C' (although there are several exceptions to even this simple rule).

No doubt there is something of an overlap between mnemonics and a situation when a speller remembers to exaggerate the enunciation of words like *WedNESday* and *FebRUary* to help with the spelling. As reported above, over-enunciation in this way has been identified as helpful in the case of older spellers.

In the following chapter, the teaching of strategies will be discussed more fully, together with other advice of a practical nature.

LINKS TO MORE ON DEVELOPMENTAL STAGES AND SPELLING STRATEGIES

- Information on stages of development in spelling and on invented spelling can be located at the Reading Rockets website at: http://www.readingrockets.org/article/267
- A useful summary of developmental aspects of spelling, plus practical suggestions for teaching, can be found on the Zaner-Bloser website for Spelling Connections 2007 at: http://www.zaner-bloser.com/WorkArea/showcontent.aspx?id=4826
- A comprehensive list of spelling strategies is available online from the Department of Education in Tasmania (2007) at: http://wwwfp.education.tas.gov.au/english/spellstrat.htm
- More on spelling strategies at: http://www.everydayspelling.com/reference/refstrategies.html and http://www.macmillan-academy.org.uk/Navigation/CC/Lit/spelling.html
- Advice and ideas for spelling instruction are provided by Zutell online at: http://www.zaner-bloser.com/educator/products/spelling/index.aspx?id=4820&view=article

four

General issues in teaching spelling

KEY ISSUES

- The teaching of spelling is a responsibility for all teachers, regardless of subject specialisation.
- All schools should have a written policy on spelling instruction that is understood and implemented by all teachers.
- Teachers need guidance on what to teach, in terms of priority vocabulary and word study strategies.
- Teachers also need guidance on time allocation and organisation options for teaching spelling.
- Assistive technology has an important role to play in fostering students' writing and spelling ability.

Many years ago, in the context of Australian primary schools, I (Westwood, 1979, p. 1) wrote:

> Teachers seem uncertain of how to proceed in order to advance the spelling skills of their students. Some feel that very little specific teaching of spelling will be needed provided the children read and write a great deal within the range of their own experience, thoughts and interests. In other words, some teachers believe that spelling will be caught through incidental learning and need not be taught. At the other extreme, some teachers deal with spelling almost too systematically and still apply rote

learning approaches and the learning of rules to a daily or weekly word list, regardless of whether the students ever need to use those words in their writing. Somewhere between the extremes a sensible balance exists for most students.

Since 1979, very many changes have occurred in the teaching of literacy in primary and secondary schools; methods have come and gone – but I could still make precisely the same observation about the teaching of spelling today. As indicated in Chapter 1, teachers remain confused about how best to deal with this mechanical aspect of the writing process. This chapter raises some general issues to help throw light on this subject.

School policy and cross-curricular aspects

In the same way that *all* teachers should be teachers of reading and all teachers should be teachers of numeracy, so too all teachers should be teachers of spelling. Students are required to write in virtually all school subjects, and all teachers are therefore in a position to provide students with corrective feedback and guidance on spelling and other aspects of their writing. It is not the sole responsibility of the teachers of English. Schools that wisely prepare an agreed policy about instruction in spelling across the year groups usually make reference to this cross-curricular aspect of spelling and point out that all teachers must involve themselves in guiding students' development. This is particularly the case in secondary schools where several different teachers may teach a particular class of students. A school policy can contain guidance for teachers on adopting a common approach to teaching spelling, setting consistent standards, identifying students' errors, and how such errors are to be corrected by the students.

It is very beneficial for the staff of any school to devote some staff-meeting time occasionally to discussing and sharing beliefs about the importance (or otherwise) of accurate spelling, and how the teaching and correction of spelling should be approached. It was precisely in that way that I first became interested in the issue of spelling more than 40 years ago. In 1966, the principal of the secondary school where I was a teaching devoted several staff meetings over a school term to the topic. From these meetings we developed a school policy that was understood, accepted and enacted by teachers across all disciplines.

Spelling in the primary school

Children acquire most of their spelling skills during the primary school years, with spelling ability developing alongside reading and phonics in a mutually supportive manner. Standardised tests of spelling ability show quite clearly that there is a rapid growth of spelling ability from age 6 years to around 12+ years (Westwood & Bissaker, 2005). The rate of development slows significantly in the secondary school years, mainly because students have by that time acquired their core spelling vocabulary for everyday writing purposes and are adding to it only new vocabulary from school subjects, world news, reading and the media. Obviously, the major thrust for teaching spelling must therefore occur in the primary school.

Three main issues arise for primary school teachers: (a) What body of words should be studied? (b) Which skills and strategies should be taught? (c) How much time should be allocated to spelling instruction? (d) How should it be organised? These issues are interrelated and need careful consideration.

What to teach?

In recent years, teachers have been able to obtain some guidance about content for a spelling program from the specific objectives for spelling that are usually contained within the curriculum guidelines and frameworks provided in relevant official documents; for example, *English: A curriculum profile for Australian schools* (Curriculum Corporation, 1994), *Benchmarks for literacy* (Curriculum Corporation, 2000); and, in the United Kingdom, the *National Curriculum: English* (DfCSF, 2002). The detail provided in the *Benchmarks for Literacy* document is considerably more than in the other documents and is potentially most helpful for teachers (see the Links box at the end of the chapter for details).

Often the objectives, attainment targets or standards included in curriculum guidelines tend to be quite general statements and do not, in themselves, provide sufficient detail for classroom planning purposes. For example, the *National Curriculum* in the United Kingdom takes a developmental approach and states that at Level 1 (i.e., the most basic), children begin to understand spelling using sound–symbol relationships and can produce some predictable letter strings. At Level 2, monosyllabic words are usually spelt correctly and where there are inaccuracies, the alternative is usually phonetically plausible. From Level 2 to Level 5 they build steadily on this understanding and can spell increasingly complex words. From Level 6 to Level 8 children develop their independence in spelling and are able to spell unfamiliar words and to check the accuracy of what they write (QCA, 2007). The 'levels' refer to stages of development and are not equated with age or grade levels; for example, a student aged 12 with spelling difficulties may still be at Level 2. To compensate for the lack of clear guidelines on what to teach, the Literacy Trust in the United Kingdom has prepared suggested word lists covering the first five years of schooling, to accompany the *National Literacy Strategy* (see the Links box at the end of the chapter).

Many schools use official guidelines as a starting point and produce their own more detailed curriculum documents that describe precisely the knowledge and skills students are expected to attain at each year level. Often these school-based resources also incorporate practical ideas for teaching. For example, staff of Albuera Street Primary School, Hobart (2004) developed an excellent scope and sequence document for instruction in spelling based on general principles from the *Learning, teaching and assessment guide* of the Department of Education, Tasmania.

The traditional source of words for spelling were grade-level word lists, often produced by education departments; but Nugent (2005) correctly points out that spelling lists all but disappeared in the 1980s and 1990s when the whole-language approach was at the height of its popularity. This situation has left teachers uncertain of what content to focus on if they do decide to attempt to teach spelling. Mostly, they follow the principle of helping each child with his or her personal spelling needs while writing. This is sometimes supplemented with the occasional 'mini lesson' in which a particular rule or word family might be explored by the whole class. A few teachers, to reassure themselves that they are at least tackling spelling more systematically within the whole-language classroom, revert back to the use of grade-level word lists or commercially produced spelling programs, but expect children to learn the words mainly through memorisation (Westwood, 2005). There is very little benefit from such an approach because word lists are rarely connected with students' immediate writing needs. Grade-level lists also ignore the developmental differences in spelling ability among students in the same grade.

Although the use of lists became unpopular, there is still much value in using certain types of list. For example, a list of the most commonly used words in children's writing (a core vocabulary list) is fully justified (see Appendix 1). Learning to spell these words correctly and automatically should be a very high priority for all students. If they master this relatively small bank of words, they will make far fewer errors in their writing and will find the task much less daunting (Graham et al., 1994; Roberts, 2001). Other lists may illustrate words that share orthographic units in common (word families) or depict particular morphemic principles. Vocabulary lists for each new topic or theme in the general curriculum can also be introduced and displayed in large-size poster format in the classroom. Ideally, each student would also be provided with a copy. Students can build lists of words that will serve their own writing needs and which they can use as a point of reference when writing and proofreading (Bean, 1998). Such lists might cover words the students need to use regularly and lists of their own spelling 'demons'. Teachers need to ensure that students understand the value of using such lists for checking their own written work, and that they acquire the habit of doing so (Thibodeau, 2002).

Skills and strategies

The real value of providing valid word lists in the classroom comes from using them to teach children *how* to learn words. For example, children should be helped, through explicit teaching, to decide whether a particular word in a list is most easily mastered by attending to the syllables and sounds (the phonemic or phonetic strategy), by remembering its visual appearance (the visual imagery strategy), by utilising information about the units of meaning that have been combined to produce the word (the morphemic strategy), by comparing the new word with one that is already known (the strategy of spelling by analogy), or by using some combination of these and other strategies (Dahl et al., 2003; Fulk 1997). As indicated in the previous chapter, almost all students have acquired a repertoire of effective and less effective strategies as a result of their experiences with reading and writing. As far as possible, teachers need to acknowledge these existing strategies and help students refine and extend them.

The teaching of spelling strategies is not restricted to word lists and can be developed through most of the activities described in the next chapter under 'word study'. Strategies can also be reinforced through feedback to students as they write and as they correct their errors. Students need frequent reminders about applying the spelling strategies they have been taught; otherwise they tend to revert to previously acquired (and often less effective) methods. In particular, students need to be reminded about using effective strategies when they take words home to learn. There is value in discussing spelling strategies with parents so that they too can encourage effective learning methods rather than mere rote memorisation.

Time allocation for spelling

Perhaps the most difficult decision for teachers to make is whether to allocate specific blocks of time to spelling and word study, or whether to incorporate this teaching in a less formal manner within every literacy lesson, as whole language advocates suggest. In the primary school years it is necessary to do both. It is ideal to combine intensive word study (in periods devoted specifically to it) with individual guidance while children write and correct their work. Suggestions for activities to use within the allocated time are presented in the next chapter.

In the early primary school years, there is every reason to allocate specific time to spelling. In the United Kingdom, the daily 'literacy hour', introduced as part of the *National Literacy Strategy*, specifically recommends using approximately 15 minutes of that hour for word and sentence study. An expert on children's spelling, Richard Gentry (2001; 2004), also advises using at least 15 minutes regularly during language arts lessons for word study and spelling. It is also pertinent to point out that all commercially produced spelling programs (e.g., *Spelling through morphographs*, Dixon & Engelmann, 1976, and *THRASS*, Davies & Ritchie, 2004) naturally require about 20 minutes devoted to intensive work every day. It is only with this degree of intensity and frequency that real benefits are likely to accrue (Carmichael & Hempenstall, 2006).

In addition to the separate time devoted to word study and spelling, teachers will of course continue to help students at an individual level while they are writing. But it is impossible for students to learn all that there is to learn about the logic of spelling by occasional guidance and corrective feedback alone. Such an individualised approach lacks necessary intensity and focus. Learning words in isolation while writing does not guarantee that the words will be remembered; nor does it result in a student gaining awareness of spelling principles and commonalities among words. For example, a teacher rarely has time to point out to a student that a word just used in a story follows a particular spelling principle or belongs to a family of other words sharing the same orthographic unit – and attempting to do this would disrupt the writing and composing process anyway.

As children reach the upper primary and middle school years, the need for separate time allocation reduces because the basic principles and concepts for spelling have been established. The most common approach in upper primary school is for the teacher to set aside a brief period of time on several occasions in each week to focus on interesting words from the students' own writing, or words that are related to some of the subjects and themes studied within the curriculum (Chandler, 2000; Yetter, 2001).

Organisation

Interactive whole-class teaching is perhaps the most effective way of conducting the sessions of word study and spelling (DfEE, 1998). This approach aims to generate a very high level of attention, engagement and active participation by students. Positive learning occurs because students are cognitively active in processing and using relevant information, expressing it in their own words, working with it and receiving immediate feedback. While the teacher controls the lesson fairly tightly, the students contribute their own ideas, express their opinions, ask questions and explain their thinking to others (Dickinson, 2003; Hardman et al., 2003). Learning is not achieved by adopting a simplistic formula of a mini lecture followed by 'drill and practice', or by expecting students to teach themselves from spelling exercises in books or from other materials. The activities used within the interactive lesson help students understand spelling principles, gain confidence in analysing words and acquire additional strategies for spelling.

The disadvantage of whole-class teaching is that it ignores individual differences among students in terms of their spelling ability and needs. It is suggested by some authorities that spelling instruction should be differentiated so that students study words that are developmentally appropriate, and receive instruction according to their developmental level (Invernizzi & Hayes, 2004). This suggestion is sound in principle, but is far from easy to do in a large class. Differentiation can be achieved to some degree by using computer-assisted learning with spelling materials at different levels of difficulty, and also by encouraging class-wide peer tutoring, with children helping one another on spelling assignments (see Chapter 6).

Spelling in secondary schools

All teachers of specialist subjects can be encouraged to prepare core vocabulary lists that contain the common terminology of their own subject. Such a list can then be provided to all students in their classes with the expectation that they will be able to read those terms, know their meaning, and spell them accurately when writing. Duplicate copies of this list can be kept inside each student's exercise book and referred to when he or she is proofreading assignments. A more general word list containing the most frequently used words in all types of writing should be given to students who have spelling difficulties. In addition, every student can be required to compile a personal spelling list that contains the words that he or she finds difficult. Again, a copy of that list can be retained in the back of every exercise book to facilitate self-correction of errors.

Teachers of English may decide to give some attention to word study on a fairly regular basis. The focus will usually be on morphological and etymological aspects, and extending students' general vocabulary. Often the source of words for study will be the complex literature that students are encountering.

Teachers with a responsibility for students with learning difficulties will certainly need to provide additional support for spelling. Many of the activities described in the following two chapters can be adapted so they are appropriate for adolescent students. In particular, students will need to be taught coping strategies so that they can compensate for their weaker spelling ability by using recognised sources of assistance, such as peers, a dictionary, or a spell-checker.

Arousing students' interest in words

One of the main findings from research over the past 20 years is that children make most progress in spelling when their teachers manage to arouse their genuine interest in words (e.g., Martins & Silva, 2006; O'Sullivan, 2000; Sipe, 2001). I can recall visiting a primary classroom in the district of Taperoo, South Australia, where the teacher displayed a remarkable talent in this respect. The atmosphere of the classroom was one in which words were seen as important, interesting and worthy of careful study. The walls of her classroom were papered with new vocabulary that had emerged from each day's lessons. She encouraged her students to compare and contrast words, to use the dictionary or to carry out an online search to check the meanings of words, to take a base word and discover how many other words could be derived from it, and to assist one another with daily spelling needs. Her students produced their own personal dictionaries and took responsibility for (and pride in) checking and self-correcting their own spelling as well as receiving corrective feedback from the teacher. Adequate time and attention were devoted to this important aspect of literacy. Students were learning essential habits for attending more closely to words, and at the same time gaining a deeper understanding of a system that would help their spelling skills transfer and generalise. As Hammond (2004, p. 11) suggests, an effective spelling program ensures that children really do, in her words, 'construct their understanding of English orthography'.

Several studies have highlighted the importance of helping young children become intrinsically interested in words and then providing them with the skills necessary for analysing words as an aid to spelling. Martins and Silva (2006), for example, worked with children aged 5 to 6 years, using activities to encourage them to think about how words may be reduced to component parts. Encouraging children to 'have a go' at writing words by inventing their spelling was found to be an important way of encouraging awareness of the oral and aural segmentation of words. The researchers suggest that the process by which children search for the best letters with which to match sounds in a word fosters an essential *analytic attitude* towards words.

Sipe (2001) stresses the fact that teachers must play an active role in helping children think about word structure, letter clusters, rhyme and analogy in order to foster optimum spelling development. Canado (2006), working with primary school students learning English as a foreign language, stressed the immense value of helping them notice key features of words. Canado refers to this important focus as *consciousness-raising*, and states that, 'Merely drawing the students' conscious attention to certain orthographic rules and patterns, and a little time spent explicitly working with these spelling aspects (15 to 20 minutes, twice a week), clearly helped develop orthographic abilities' (Canado, 2006, p. 35). Overall, this study found evidence of long-term gains from explicit instruction, and also reinforced the notion that abundant practice is essential for spelling improvement.

Helping children become interested in word structure by having them identify groups of letters shared by different words, deducing any rules that may be operating in particular word families, and using this information to decode and spell unfamiliar words is the principal aim of what is called the 'investigative approach' to spelling. Under this approach, spelling is seen as a problem-solving activity. Poulter (2002, p. 11) explains the rationale in these terms:

> An investigative and problem-solving approach helps pupils become more confident about unknown words. They realise that the English language has some rules that are useful and many that are broken. Perhaps more importantly, children become interested in words, more enthusiastic about the vocabulary they encounter in all areas of life, and more prepared to have a go at spelling them.

Assistive technology

Studies using assistive technology for spelling instruction or remediation (e.g. word processors, spell-checkers, computer software programs) have yielded mainly positive results (Hetzroni & Shrieber, 2004; Hilte et al., 2005; Lewis et al., 1998; Vedora & Stromer, 2007; Wanzek et al., 2006). For example, Torgerson and Elbourne (2002) concluded that the use of computer software to teach spelling may be as effective as conventional forms of teaching; and for students with motivational problems, it may be preferable because they find it more engaging than other modes of delivery.

Many software packages designed to develop spelling skills are available. Teachers should ensure that the way in which the words are presented on the screen causes the students to attend carefully to the complete sequence of letters and to the orthographic sub-units within words. Responses should require the student to type the complete word from memory each time. Programs that focus too much attention on spelling letter-by-letter, inserting missing letters into spaces, or untangling jumbled words are far less effective.

The keyboarding-spelling connection

In Chapter 2, reference was made to the association between handwriting and spelling, with a conclusion that the action of writing helps students store orthographic patterns in long-term memory. It may be that keyboarding practice has a similar effect. For example, Whiting and Chapman (2000) reported positively on the outcomes from a carefully sequenced touch-typing, spelling and reading program used with students aged 8 to 16 years.

These researchers hypothesised that the nature of the learning activity helps students internalise correct spelling patterns. The sequential, repetitive process needed to learn touch-typing may aid the learning of important orthographic patterns of English.

Spell-checkers

Several studies have explored the value of spell-checkers for students with spelling difficulties (e.g., MacArthur et al., 1996). Most spell-checkers associated with word processors are generally helpful in that they usually highlight incorrect spellings; however, one must be a fairly proficient reader and an adequate speller in order to use them effectively and independently. For students with severe reading and spelling difficulties, a spell-checker is not always of much assistance because their attempt at typing the word produced an error that could not be recognised by the computer (Jackson et al., 2003; Montgomery et al., 2001). They may also have trouble reading the alternative spellings displayed by the computer. According to the study carried out by MacArthur et al. (1996), only approximately one-quarter of errors are recognised by a computer. This is partly due to the problem identified above, but also relates to the computer's inability to detect the incorrect use of a word which has the correct spelling (e.g. *there* in place of *their*; *how* instead of *who*, *red* instead of *read*).

Another difficulty arises for the student who is a very poor reader. Students need to be able to understand the instructions associated with the spell-checker. For example, one of my students in a learning support group misunderstood the instruction 'add' when it appeared among the options *ignore, ignore all, add, change, change all, autocorrect*. He clicked on '*add*', hoping that the correct spelling would then be added to his text. What happened, of course, was that the incorrect word was added to computer's memory-bank. After several weeks, the computer had stored many incorrect spellings and was no longer highlighting his spelling errors! It is clear that students with learning difficulties require careful instruction and close monitoring in the effective use of a spell-checker (Ashton, 1999).

Students with learning difficulties

Much of the research in assistive technology has focused on students with learning disabilities, using the technology to improve their writing and spelling. Computers can help students with learning difficulties because the style of presentation holds the students' attention, involves active learning, provides for adequate practice, gives immediate feedback, and the level of the work can be adjusted to each student's ability and learning rate (Minton, 2002).

Some of the research using computer presentation methods for spelling has also incorporated a procedure known as 'constant time delay' (CTD). CTD is designed to produce a very high success rate, with near error-free learning. Under CTD conditions a voice on the computer may say a target word (e.g. 'Spell *horse*'). At first the word 'horse' appears on the screen at the same time the word is pronounced, and the student writes or types it. In subsequent sessions, the word will be pronounced and will not appear on the screen until 5 seconds later, allowing time for the student to attempt the spelling of the word independently. This computer-based approach with CTD has proved very successful (Cates et al., 2007; Coleman-Martin & Heller, 2004).

LINKS TO MORE ON ISSUES IN SPELLING INSTRUCTION

- Recommended spelling lists associated with the National Literacy Strategy in the United Kingdom for children in Reception to Year 5 classes are available online at: http://www.literacytrust.org.uk/Database/Primary/NLSwords.html
- The 100 most commonly used words in English writing are online at: http://www.literacytrust.org.uk/Database/100_words.html
- Attainment targets for spelling within the National Curriculum in the United Kingdom. Go first to National Curriculum Online. Select 'English'. Then click on 'attainment targets' and then finally on 'E3 Writing'. http://www.nc.uk.net/webdav/harmonise?Page/@id=6004&Subject/@id=5985
- The spelling standards from Australian Benchmarks for Literacy can be accessed online at: http://online.curriculum.edu.au/litbench/build.asp?pg=8
- Useful word lists covering general writing needs and specific spelling vocabulary for different specialist subjects within the school curriculum can be located online at: http://www.phon.ucl.ac.uk/home/dick/tta/spelling/ks3list.htm

five

Activities for teaching and learning

KEY ISSUES

- Spelling skills need to be taught alongside instruction in word recognition and phonic decoding.
- Children benefit greatly from opportunities to study words and discover similarities, differences, rules and exceptions to rules. In particular, children need to move beyond single-letter phonic decoding to reach the stage of recognising and applying larger orthographic units.
- Teaching should aim to provide each and every student with a repertoire of effective spelling and checking strategies.
- Time also needs to be devoted to mastering a core vocabulary of words frequently required in everyday writing.

There are three main aims for teaching spelling in the primary school years:

- to help students develop awareness of the guiding principles that influence English spelling, and to become familiar with functional orthographic units
- to provide students with a repertoire of strategies for studying and learning new words, and for proofreading, checking and correcting errors
- to ensure that students acquire automatic recall of the spelling of commonly used words needed in everyday writing, many of which do not have regular graphophonic characteristics.

Developing students' awareness of spelling principles and components

The most basic principle that children must understand at a very early stage is that the spelling of most words can be determined by attending to the component sounds that make up that word when it is spoken, and that these sounds can be represented by letters written in sequence (Wanzek et al., 2006). This is referred to as the phonic principle. Most young children, as explained earlier, begin to discover this principle for themselves, as evidenced by their attempts at invented spelling. Other children require explicit instruction to reach the same level of understanding. For all children, early spelling skills are accelerated when word recognition, phonics, spelling and writing are taught together in an integrated manner (Cates et al., 2007; Noell et al., 2006). Successful published programs for developing basic literacy (e.g., *THRASS*, Davies & Ritchie, 2004) recognise the need for making clear the connections between spelling, reading and phonics.

As children gain experience with listening to, thinking about, reading and writing words, their control over the alphabetic code rapidly increases. Orthographic knowledge is acquired as they gain this experience, and they begin to make generalisations about the kinds of letter sequences that can occur together within the language (Senechal et al., 2006).

Teaching basic phonics

Teaching phonics means teaching children the relationships between speech sounds (phonemes) and letters, and how to use this knowledge to read and spell words. It is now agreed that children should not be left to discover the phonic principle merely through incidental learning, but rather that the teaching of phonics should be done explicitly, systematically and early (Mesmer & Griffith, 2006). Research appears to favour the approach called *synthetic phonics* in which children are first taught to associate a letter or group of letters with a corresponding sound and then to use this knowledge to read and spell words (Johnston & Watson, 2005). The 'synthesis' aspect of the method involves the ability to blend the separate sound units together to produce the word in speech or writing.

Letter-to-sound correspondences may be introduced in any order; in practice, the order is often dictated by the nature of the reading materials the children are using and the writing they are doing each day. One systematic approach begins by selecting highly contrastive sounds such as /m/, /k/, /v/ and avoiding confusable sounds such as /m/ and /n/, or /p/ and /b/. It is also helpful to teach first the most consistent letter–sound associations (Heilman, 2006). Vowel sounds are far less consistent than consonants in their letter-to-sound correspondences. After first establishing the most common vowel sound associations (/a/ as in *apple*, /e/ as in *egg*, /i/ as in *ink*, /o/ as in *orange* and /u/ as in *up*), variations are best learned later, in combination with other letters when words containing these units are encountered (e.g. *–ar–*, *–aw–*, *-ie-*, *–ee–*, *–ea–*, *–ai–*, etc.).

Simple word-building experience

Although children may well be attempting to invent the spelling of much more complex words in their daily writing, for teaching purposes it is advisable to practise word building and word analysis at a simple level to ensure a high success rate. This can be achieved by introducing onset-rime activities, both orally and in writing. *Onset* is the term applied to the initial sound in a single-syllable word, while *rime* refers to the remaining unit that contains the vowel and other letters; for example, in the word *shop,* /sh/ is the onset and /op/ is the rime. Rime units are the basis for most 'word families' such as *lick, sick, kick, pick, wick, stick, trick, thick, brick,* etc. These letter groups represent the important early orthographic units that children will need to master.

Onset-rime activities can be devised to help children understand that spoken words can be reduced to smaller parts. Being able to break single-syllable words into onset and rime is the starting point for more demanding word analysis and segmentation later. The following common rime units can be used to build more than 650 one-syllable words (Glass et al., 2000). Young children's interest can be aroused by challenging them to make as many real words as possible from some of these units.

–ay	–ill	–at	–am	–ag	–ack	–ank	–ick	–ell	–ot
–ing	–ap	–unk	–ail	–ain	–eed	–y	–out	–ug	
–op	–in	–an	–est	–ink	–ow	–ew	–ore	–ed	–ab
–ob	–ock	–ake	–ine	–ight	–im	–uck	–um	–ust	

Onset and rime activities should also be used a little later to encourage blending with consonant digraphs and blends, and to reinforce other orthographic units. For example:

Make the sounds and say the words.

```
sw:    –im,   –ing,  –ell,   –eep
ch:    –eer,  –in,   –op,    –urch
str:   –ong,  –ing,  –ike,   –ap
–ck:   ba–,   de–,   ro–,    du–
–tch:  ma–,   wa–,   ca–,    fe–,   no–,   pa–,   sti–,  di–,   pi–,   hi–
```

After tackling the list orally, students can be invited to say, and then write, the words.

For the highest level of proficiency in recognising and spelling unfamiliar words, students need experience in working with longer and more complex orthographic units such as: *–eed, –ide, –ight, –ound, –own, –ous, –ough, –tion,* etc. Bhattacharya (2006) points out that being able to break complex words into pronounceable sub-units of this type is important even for older students when dealing with difficult terminology in subject textbooks such as science and geography.

It must be remembered that all word-building activities are used as supplements to reading and writing for real purposes, *not as a replacement* for authentic literacy experiences. Much phonic knowledge can be taught or reinforced from the words students are reading in their books or attempting to write (Pullen et al., 2005). As far as possible, phonic knowledge and spelling skills should not be taught and practised totally out of context. While students do need specific time devoted to mastering phonic units and working with word families, every effort must be made to ensure that this learning is quickly applied to 'real' reading and writing.

Word study

Word study has been defined as 'planned and directed instruction and practice of English sounds, words and syllable patterns combined with vocabulary development' (Frank, 2007, p. 1). It is known to build confidence in tackling the spelling of difficult and unfamiliar words, and can be tailored to the ability level and needs of particular age groups, including adults (Holmes & Malone, 2004). For adults, Massengill (2006) describes an 'Interactive Word Study' approach that helps students examine, compare, discriminate and make judgements about letter sequences needed to represent units of sound and meaning. Over time, the activities helped less able spellers internalise and generalise key features of spelling patterns. Massengill also remarks that having been exposed to the word study approach these mature individuals reported gains in confidence in their own ability to spell difficult words.

Word study is one of the essential features of an effective spelling program (Barone, 1992). The activity belongs generally under the category 'investigative approach'. The advantage claimed for word study is that it provides useful knowledge that can be generalised to the spelling of other words. Joseph and Orlins (2005) state that word study and 'word sorting' are key ways of encouraging an analytic approach to words and helping spellers develop awareness of orthographic units.

Word families

Word families are groups of words that share common visual, phonologic or morphemic features. Some teachers highlight the relevant orthographic units in colour. Examples include:

(visual) *cough, tough, rough, enough, though, through*
(phonologic) *light, sight, might, right, fight, tight, night, fright, flight, slight / bite, rite, cite, mite, kite, site, white, quite*
(morphemic) *certain, uncertain, uncertainty, certainly*

Other families may comprise words that are exceptions to a rule, words that illustrate a rule and words that contain a silent letter. After studying a particular word family, it is valuable to display the words on the classroom wall for reference, and to return to them occasionally.

Gaining experience in reading words within word families, noting similarities and differences, spelling the words from dictation and using the words within daily writing contexts is extremely useful to overall spelling development (Johnston, 1999). It is one of the ways in which students are helped to grasp the principle of spelling by analogy through recognising the common orthographic patterns shared by many words.

Word sorting

Word sorting is an activity designed to stimulate students' analytical thinking. Invernizzi et al. (1994) comment that students benefit from the opportunity to examine, manipulate and make decisions about words according to categories of similarity and difference. Bhattacharya and Ehri (2004) and Chandler (2000) suggest that comparing and contrasting words helps older students discover basic spelling rules. For example, comparing *tapped*, *tapping* and *hopped*, *hopping* with *taped*, *taping*, *hoped*, *hoping* enables students to recognise the principle of doubling the final consonant when adding 'ed' or 'ing' to certain words.

The words to be studied and compared are provided on separate cards. For example, at a fairly simple level the words might be:

---

back, sock, black, suck, pluck, truck, lock, rack, kick, track, trick, block, brick, lick, rock, sack, pack

---

The students are asked to sort the word cards into categories. They are asked, 'What is the *same* about these words?' The response might be that they all end in 'ck'; or that they are regular words and can be spelled as they sound. 'What is *different* about some of the words?' The response might be that the vowel is different; or that some words use four letters and the other five letters; or that some words begin with consonant blends, others with a single consonant. The words can, however, be categorised in other ways too. After studying the word, the students are invited to think of other words that could be added to any of the categories they have created; and they test one another on the spelling of some of the words on the cards.

At higher levels, the students might be working with *–ation* words, for example:

---

dictation, presentation, invitation, nation, station, relation, equation, demonstration

---

Or they might be studying the way in which vowel sounds are frequently modified by the consonant that follows them. Selection of the actual words for study should be made relative to the students' developmental spelling stage.

The use of word sorting is strongly supported by Joseph and McCachran (2003) as a valuable means of helping students recognise important letter patterns within and across words. Zutell (1998) states that middle primary school students introduced to word sorting showed positive changes in their spelling strategies, were enthusiastic about engaging in the activity and indicated improved ability to use information about letter patterns to edit their own writing. Word study and word sorting are ways of encouraging an analytic approach to words and to develop awareness of orthographic units.

In a mixed-ability class, it is important not to allow group activities involving word sorting (or other investigative activities) to be dominated by the students who are already proficient spellers. Ideally, the words allocated to different groups will be differentiated according to students' developmental level and ability.

One version of word sorting and word analysis is known as the *Directed Spelling Thinking Activity (DSTA)* (Graham et al., 1996). *DSTA* is a word-study procedure in which the students work in groups to analyse two or more words based on points of similarity or difference. For example, the students may explore words containing the long /a/ sound, as in *pail*, *male* and *pay*. They discover that different letter combinations can represent the same sound. The students are then given lists of words (or they search for words themselves) to classify as belonging or not belonging in a similar category. Follow-up activities include looking for words containing a specific orthographic unit within their reading material. Over a period of time lists of words that follow a particular rule, or are exceptions to that rule, are constructed, displayed in the classroom and used regularly for revision.

Dictation

Although it has remained popular in the context of teaching English as a second language, the use of dictation exercises fell out of favour in regular English classes in primary and secondary schools some years ago. The main criticisms were that it was used only to test students not teach them, it was artificial and it was boring. However, dictation exercises have definite value and can be used to advance students' spelling and proofreading skills (Lightfoot, 2005). The best format for dictation involves the following principles:

- Select an interesting passage that is at an appropriate level of difficulty.
- Allow time for students to study the passage briefly before closing the book. This enables them to identify any difficult words and to seek clarification of the meaning of any new vocabulary.
- Encourage students to listen attentively while the passage is dictated, and remind them to apply relevant spelling strategies.
- Give ample time for students to check and self-correct their work before marking.
- Use the errors that are made by students as a focus for further instruction.

Used in this way, dictation helps students concentrate on careful listening and give full attention to accuracy in spelling. The approach also encourages proofreading and self-correction. Teachers sometimes ask students to exchange their work for checking; but it is important not to embarrass weaker spellers by this process.

Explicit teaching of spelling strategies

Senechal et al. (2006) remind us that learning to spell involves developing efficient and flexible strategies. Strategic spellers are able, when necessary, to call upon several sources of information for encoding and checking unfamiliar words. Teaching students to use effective strategies is one of the main goals of instruction in spelling (Lam & Westwood, 2006).

Although most students have developed a number of spelling strategies for themselves, often these strategies are insufficient to meet all their needs in striving for accurate spelling (Rittle-Johnson & Siegler, 1999). The teacher's role is to extend their existing repertoire by encouraging, for example, greater use of visual imagery, employing spelling by analogy, using over-enunciation to highlight tricky points within a word, thinking of word meanings to help decide on a spelling and even devising mnemonics to overcome certain spelling demons.

As indicated in Chapter 3, effective instruction in spelling involves not only teaching knowledge about words (phonemic, graphophonic and morphemic), but also teaching specific strategies that students can use when learning to spell an unfamiliar word. The explicit teaching sequence described below can be applied to any of the specific strategies described in Chapter 3, namely:

- spell it as it sounds
- look-say-cover-write-check
- spelling by analogy
- using morphemes
- over-enunciation
- recitation.

Strategies are usually taught most effectively when the teacher demonstrates very clearly how he or she approaches the task of spelling or checking a word. 'Thinking aloud' is the standard way of showing students how they might apply a given strategy for a given purpose. Having demonstrated the strategy at least three times, and having discussed its value – where and when it would be useful – students are then required to apply the strategy themselves for learning appropriate target words provided by the teacher. During this guided practice stage, the teacher monitors closely what the students are doing and provides encouragement and immediate feedback. Later, students are required to demonstrate their use of the strategy without guidance and with delayed feedback. Finally, because teachers know that students will not necessarily remember always to apply a newly acquired strategy, frequent review and additional practice are always provided over a period of weeks.

In addition to the six main strategies listed above for learning new words, effective self-regulating strategies for spelling unfamiliar words usually involve teaching students to ask themselves a series of questions. For example:

- Do I know this word? Say the word. Say the word again and stretch it out.
- How many syllables can I hear? How many sounds?
- Do I know any other words that sound almost the same?
- How are those words written?
- Does this word I have written look right?
- No? I'll try it again.
- Does this look better?

Fulk (1996) used the following five-step strategy very successfully with learning disabled students. It has wide applicability, including use with adults. The strategy is particularly helpful when attempting to learn a word that does not conform to phonemic or morphemic principles (for example, a word imported into English from a foreign language). Having selected a target word for study:

- Say the word.
- Write and say the word.
- Check the spelling.
- Trace and say the word.
- Write the word from memory and check.

Proofreading and error correction

To become an independent writer and speller, students need to acquire skill in proofreading their own work and self-correcting their errors. This is never an easy process because it requires the reader to move away from the powerful influence of context in what is being read in order to give careful attention to the actual letters and words on the page. Teachers need to encourage students to check their own work carefully and to help one another with such checking and correction. Students should be praised for every attempt they make to self-correct any errors.

According to Kervin (2002), proofreading can actually be a powerful strategy for developing children's spelling ability because it causes them to attend closely and thoughtfully to letter sequences and take responsibility for accuracy. Wirtz et al. (1996) reported a small-scale study in which third-grade students were taught to use proofreading marks (such as 'wrong letter', 'letter missing') when correcting their spelling errors from a dictated list. The students then wrote the correct version of each word. They made better gains than students who simply copied the correction for each word several times and used the word in a sentence. These students also reported that they liked the method.

To become more effective proofreaders, students need the teacher to model the process clearly, using the overhead projector, whiteboard/blackboard, or prepared sheets of text (Bean, 1998). For example, students can be shown how to do the following:

- Use a strip of paper or a ruler to cover all text except for the line you are checking.
- Read slowly, word by word.
- Underline lightly any word that needs to be checked.
- Write two or more versions of a word and then decide which one looks correct.
- Use one's personal self-help checklist to detect and correct common errors.
- Exchange writing with a partner for proofreading purposes.
- Teach some of the typical symbols used by editors to signal changes needed in the text.

When teachers require students to correct spelling errors, they are hoping that by doing so the students will learn to spell those words correctly. This is unlikely to happen automatically, and routine writing of corrections ten times each is fairly futile. In determining which words should be corrected, the teacher should differentiate among students by (a) taking into account the age and ability level of the student; and (b) considering the relative importance of the words in terms of their frequency in everyday writing. Studies have suggested that no more than three words should be corrected at any one session, and that each word should be written no more than three times (Schlagal, 2002). For the writing of corrections to have any impact on students' learning, it is essential that they have every intention of trying to remedy the error and that they are attending fully to the task.

Students should transfer the correct spelling of any important words to their own personal spelling list (Manning & Underbakke, 2005). This list can be used when students are completing written assignments or checking homework.

Mastering a core of high-frequency words

Although the use of phonic knowledge is very helpful in spelling (or approximating the spelling) of more than 80 per cent of words in the English language, there are still some words that defy simple translation from sounds to letters. Unfortunately for spellers, many of the most commonly occurring words that they require in their written language fall into this category. A glance at the word list in Appendix 1 reveals that many of these words cannot be written by reference only to their phonemes. Nor is morphemic information of assistance in spelling these irregular words. They have to be mastered by visual and motor methods (i.e., frequent writing or typing). Once they are mastered, students make many fewer errors in everyday writing (Graham et al., 1994; 1996; Roberts, 2001).

To utilise a visual memory approach for learning common but irregular words, one of the simplest aids to make and use is the flashcard. Words are introduced to the student on cards about 30 cm × 10 cm. The word is pronounced clearly and attention is drawn to any particular features in the printed word that may be difficult to recall later. The student is encouraged to make a 'mental picture' of the word, and examine it. Some teachers say, 'Use your eyes like a camera. Take a picture of the word. Close your eyes and imagine you can still see the word.' With eyes closed, the student is then told to trace the word in the air. After a few seconds the student writes the word from memory. The word is then checked against the flashcard. The writing of the whole word avoids the inefficient letter-by-letter copying habit that some students have developed. If there is no error, move to the next target word. If an error has been made, show the card again, then remove it and the student makes another attempt at writing the word from memory. This method is, of course, simply a variation of the look-say-cover-write-check learning strategy discussed in Chapter 3.

Repeated writing of a target word can also be very helpful in establishing the core vocabulary of irregular words if the student is attending fully to the task. It is one way in which kinaesthetic images of words can be more firmly established. But, as stated above for writing corrections, only a few words (usually *no more than three*) should be practised in any one session (Schlagal, 2002).

LINKS TO MORE ON TEACHING AND LEARNING SPELLING

- Information for teachers on the aspects of spelling development that should be addressed under 'word study' is available online at: http://www.geocities.com/Athens/Troy/7175/word2.htm. See also http://www.phon.ucl.ac.uk/home/dick/tta/spelling/teaching.htm.

>

- For suggestions on using dictation see: Lightfoot, A. (2005). *Using dictation.* British Council: Teaching English website at: http://www.teachingenglish.org.uk/think/methodology/dictation.shtml
- Some useful and relevant principles for teaching spelling are available at: http://www.margaretkay.com/Spelling.htm
- A brief but excellent overview of spelling skill development and teaching are provided by Templeton and Morris, available in *Reading Online, 5(3)* at: http://www.readingonline.org/articles/art_index.asp?HREF=/articles/handbook/templeton/index.html
- THRASS (Teaching Handwriting, Reading and Spelling Skills) is a very useful program for developing a thorough understanding of phonic units in English language. Teachers can learn much from it, as well as their students.
  For THRASS in Australia, see http://www.thrass.com.au/research1.html
  For THRASS in the United Kingdom, see http://www.thrass.co.uk.

six

Intervention for spelling difficulties

KEY ISSUES

- Many students find spelling a difficult cognitive skill to master.
- There are many possible reasons for difficulty in learning to spell, some of them inherent in the individual and some due to adverse outside influences.
- Intervention for spelling difficulties should take account of students' current knowledge, skills and strategies and should build upon these.
- A learning disability (dysorthographia) can sometimes cause the difficulty with spelling; but it should not be regarded as a very common cause. Students with a learning disability can be helped by exactly the same remedial methods as other weak spellers.

Achieving proficiency in spelling is particularly difficult for some students. They become frustrated by their inability to spell correctly many of the words they need to write in their school assignments. Their ongoing difficulties, together with the negative criticism often received from others, can undermine their confidence and reduce their motivation for writing in the classroom.

Although there is a close connection between reading and spelling (as discussed in Chapter 2), being a good reader does not guarantee that a person is also a good speller. Spelling calls upon specific memory processes and perceptual abilities that are less important, or are used differently, in reading. Simply doing more reading does not help students to remedy their persistent spelling errors. It has been noted, for example, that individuals who are poor spellers do not recognise that they are habitually spelling a word incorrectly when they encounter that word in their reading (Holmes & Davis, 2002).

Possible causes of difficulty

Some students have perceptual or cognitive weaknesses that contribute to their problems in learning to spell; but others have simply lost their way somewhere on the route from beginning speller to independent speller. Poor spelling can sometimes be attributed to insufficient instruction or to lack of interest on the part of the learner. In a few cases, problems may be due to a combination of orthographic processing deficits within the student's cognitive architecture and poor quality teaching that has left learning to chance rather than providing clear direction (Graham et al., 2002). Some of the perceptual and cognitive deficits may relate to visual memory, phonological skills, or information processing.

Poor visual sequential memory

Weak spellers often appear to have poor memory for letter sequences, making it difficult for them to recall or 'revisualise' words or orthographic units making up those words. They also have great difficulty mastering a core spelling vocabulary of high-frequency words (Johnson & Myklebust, 1967; Lyon et al., 2003). Some weak spellers seem unable to conjure up a word image from their visual-orthographic memory, so they remain overly dependent on sound and spelling 'by ear' (Moats, 1995). A significant number of students with spelling difficulties appear to reach a plateau at the phonetic stage of spelling and remain there, unable to switch easily to apply visual imagery that would enable them to move to the next stage (Templeton, 2003). In addition, poor spellers tend to be slow at processing print, and often reverse or transpose single letters or letter groups (e.g. 'b' for 'd', *saw* for *was*, *on* for *no*, *who* for *how*). These weaknesses obviously cause major difficulties in dealing with the visual-sequential aspects of spelling.

Weak phonological skills

Phonological skills are crucial at the earliest stages of learning to spell, when young children are beginning to associate sounds with letters, but poor phonological awareness is common among weak spellers (Lyon et al., 2003; Notenboom & Reitsma, 2003). Several studies reviewed by Read and Hodges (1982) indicate that poor spellers have problems in segmenting spoken words into separate units and in learning letter–sound correspondences. Accurate identification of sounds at the ends of words appears to be particularly difficult for some students. They are reported to have major problems identifying endings such as *–ed*, *–ent*, *–er*, *–ly*, *–ally*, *–ous*, *–ent* (Moats, 1995).

When phonological training is provided, spelling skills generally improve, at least toward a higher level within the phonetic stage (Silva & Alves-Martins, 2003). Studies have tended to show that where students with spelling problems improve over time they are beginning to make better use of phonological strategies (Ball & Blachman, 1991).

Lack of morphemic knowledge

Persistent failure to spell word endings (suffixes) correctly suggests a lack of morphemic awareness. Elbro and Arnbak (1996) cite research indicating that adults who are very poor spellers tend to have limited awareness of morphemic principles.

Dixon (1991) suggested that too little instruction is given in phonemic and morphemic aspects of word study, compared with the attention given to purely visual memory methods for spelling. As stated in previous chapters, helping students understand the principles of word structure is a positive intervention for enhancing spelling ability (Nunes et al., 2006). In particular, morphological awareness facilitates the spelling of inflected and derived words (Kemp, 2006).

Restricted range of strategies

The weakest spellers seem to have a limited repertoire of strategies to use when spelling and checking words. They tend to rely on rote memorisation and recitation, rather than taking a more thoughtful and analytic approach. It is clear that they need to be taught a wider range of effective word-study strategies (Graham et al., 2002; Moats, 1995). In particular, explicit instruction should promote a fuller knowledge of the English spelling system and how it operates. Ralston and Robinson (1997) suggest that the most effective spelling intervention for a student with difficulties is one that takes into account the individual's current knowledge, skills, strategies and metacognitive processes, and builds upon them. Effective instruction does not set out to teach students how to spell every individual word they may need in their writing; rather it should teach students how to think about constructing words by drawing on the multiple linguistic factors that underlie spelling.

Dysorthographia

Students with spelling difficulties are not necessarily of low intelligence – a few may be highly intelligent. Educational psychologists suggest that some of these intelligent students have a specific learning disability termed *dysorthographia*. Their spelling difficulties may be related to underlying problems with language, memory, phonological awareness, visual processing, together with inefficient learning strategies (Plaza & Cohen, 2007; Savage & Frederickson, 2006). Cavey (2000, p. 45) states that:

> Spelling requires more auditory and visual discrimination, sequence memory, analysis and synthesis, and integration simultaneously than perhaps any other skill. Thus, the majority of children with LD have trouble spelling.

Some writers have suggested that the spelling errors made by dysorthographic students are qualitatively different from those made by other students with learning difficulties. The errors are often referred to as 'bizarre' in that there is little connection between the letters they write and sounds within the word, making it almost impossible to decode their writing (Thomson, 1995). Others have argued that the errors made by students with dysorthographia are simply typical of an earlier pre-phonemic stage on the developmental spelling continuum (Padget et al., 1996).

Dyslexia (severe reading disability) is commonly accompanied by dysorthographia and the two disabilities share some common causes. For example, lack of phonological awareness and poor visual memory are often reported in both reading and spelling disability (Johnson & Myklebust, 1967; Lyon et al., 2003). Dyslexic students have problems in rapidly naming letters, numbers and other symbols when these are presented to them (Wolf & Bowers, 1999), and it is hypothesised that this rapid naming deficit (a problem with retrieval of information from memory) may also impair rapid orthographic processing (Mather & Goldstein, 2001; Savage & Frederickson, 2006).

Intervention: basic principles

Regardless of the underlying causes, students with spelling difficulties require much more intensive, structured and explicit teaching than is necessary for their more fortunate peers (Strattman & Hodson, 2005; Vedora & Stromer, 2007; Wallace, 2006). They chiefly need abundant opportunities for writing every day with corrective feedback to ensure that spelling skills are developed. This daily writing needs to be combined with word study and explicit instruction in appropriate spelling and self-checking strategies. Graham (2000) and Richards (1999) indicate that poor spellers are not very adept at acquiring spelling skills merely through reading and other incidental means. They believe that students need to be taught effective word analysis and other strategies to help them become independent spellers. There is evidence that a brief but intensive intervention program with a focus on strategies for spelling and word analysis can have positive effects on the spelling performance and motivation of children in the primary school years (e.g., Lam & Westwood, 2006).

Some of the basic principles involved in delivering additional support to weaker spellers include:

- Arouse students' genuine interest in words. This requires teachers and tutors to display infectious enthusiasm themselves for all forms of word study and application.
- Devote adequate time to instruction in spelling. For weaker spellers in primary school, some time should be given daily to word study.
- Focus first on mastery of high-frequency words and 'easy' words that students have misspelled in their own writing.
- Limit the number of words studied each session to no more than *three* to achieve the best rate of learning and retention.
- Use multisensory response modes to motivate primary school students (e.g. writing, tracing, copying using pens of different colour, using plastic letters, keyboarding). Multisensory response may also help students assimilate and remember letter patterns.
- Use computer programs and word processors to develop positive attitudes toward drill, practice and application.
- Demonstrate effective learning strategies and provide adequate time for students to assimilate and use these strategies independently.
- Provide frequent revision and extended practice over time.

Research on spelling interventions

Since 1993, four major research reviews have reported the effectiveness of various interventions for students with poor spelling (Fulk & Stormont-Spurgin, 1995; Gordon et al., 1993; McNaughton et al., 1994; Wanzek et al., 2006). From the first three reviews, one can draw the following conclusions:

- The look-say-cover-write-check strategy is reasonably effective, if explicitly taught and thoroughly practised.
- Error modelling, in which the teacher imitates a student's error and then discusses the fault before presenting the correct response, is helpful.
- Multisensory approaches (including use of keyboard and computer) are very helpful for students with learning difficulties.
- The number of words students are required to learn consecutively should be limited.
- Presenting a stimulus word and then using time delay before revealing the correct response results in improved learning.
- Peer tutoring can be effective for raising achievement levels and as a means of providing necessary support and feedback.

The more recent review by Wanzek et al. (2006) examined in detail 19 intervention studies published between 1995 and 2003. Their main conclusion (p. 540) was that:

> Taking all of the studies into account, this synthesis revealed that spelling outcomes were consistently improved after spelling interventions that included explicit instruction with multiple practice opportunities and immediate corrective feedback after a word was misspelled.

In their review, Wanzek et al. used the statistic termed 'effect size' (ES) where possible to indicate the relative effectiveness of each approach. In analyses of research studies an ES above 0.5 is considered to be indicative of an effective intervention approach. An ES above 0.8 denotes an extremely effective approach. Using this procedure, they discovered that the most effective approach (ES = 1.76) involved a systematic program of instruction covering spelling rules, morphographic units and phoneme analysis. This intervention produced significantly better results than an approach involving the teaching of words in context and using word families (Darch et al., 2000). Fulk's (1996) study, in which students were taught a variation of look-say-cover-write-check, also produced an impressive effect size (ES = 1.25), again giving much support to this simple self-help strategy. Studies using assistive technology (e.g. word processors and spell-checkers) also yielded moderate effects (Wanzek et al., 2006).

In general, results from research have supported a view that students make most progress in spelling when they are explicitly taught effective strategies for working out how words are constructed. Intervention should help students understand the phonological and morphological principles that underpin English spelling, and should aim to establish the connection between sound units and letter groups. For example, studying families of words sharing common letter sequences and engaging in word-sorting activities are useful for this purpose (Varnhagen et al., 1992; Joseph, 2002). Moats (1995, p. 89) has reached the conclusion that:

> Spelling improvement can be brought about in poor spellers if proper instruction is carried out systematically over a long period of time, and the spelling instruction is tailored to match the developmental level of the student's word knowledge.

Specific interventions for weak spellers

It can be seen from the above reviews that some of the most common spelling strategies for use with all students, such as look-say-cover-write-check, and various activities involving word analysis have been adopted and adapted successfully for use with students exhibiting spelling difficulties. In addition, there are some corrective or compensatory intervention methods specifically designed for such students, including 'old way – new way' method, Jackson's (1994) 'Fonetik Spelling', repeated writing, and Simultaneous Oral Spelling.

Error correction: old way – new way

Weak spellers have often internalised incorrect spelling patterns and find it very difficult to replace them with correct images in long-term memory (Moats, 1995). The information the learner has already stored in memory interferes with the re-learning process due to what is termed 'proactive interference'. Grainger (1997) suggests that if young children spend too long practising incorrect spelling patterns through the use of invented spelling without corrective feedback, this can create ongoing problems for some individuals. They are storing incorrect visual images of the words as well as the incorrect motor responses. *Old way – new way* is an error-correction procedure designed to help students overcome persistent spelling errors of this kind (Lyndon, 1989).

Old way – new way uses a student's error as the starting point for intervention. The memory of the incorrect (old) way of spelling the word is used to activate an awareness of the new (correct) way of spelling the word. The following steps are followed in applying old way – new way:

- The student writes the word in the incorrect form.
- The student and teacher agree to call this the 'old way' of spelling.
- Alongside the incorrect spelling the teacher writes the new (correct) form of the word.
- Teacher and student discuss the differences between the old and new forms, e.g. *thay* and *they*. The 'a' can be crossed out and the 'e' underlined. The student says 'I used to spell it with an 'a', now I spell it with an 'e'. *They*.')
- The student writes the word again the old way.
- The student writes the word the new way and explains the difference.
- The student completes five such repetitions of old way and new way, with a verbal statement of the difference ('I used to write it with an *a*, now I write it with an *e. They.*').
- The student now writes the word six times in the new way using different size letters or different coloured chalk or pen.
- The student revises the word after a week; and again after another week.

Old way – new way has much in common with other approaches where error imitation is used as a teaching point. Error imitation, followed by modelling of correct spelling, has been identified as an effective teaching strategy in several studies (Alber & Walshe, 2004; Gordon et al., 1993; Wanzek et al., 2006).

Repeated writing

Written spelling is a physical action and the frequent writing of a word with letters in the correct sequence almost certainly helps the student establish a motor pattern for that sequence of letters in kinaesthetic memory. In much the same way, typing on a keyboard helps to establish automatic motor responses for high-frequency words. Van Hell et al. (2003) believe that the action of writing a whole word strengthens general orthographic knowledge as well as aiding retention of that word in long-term memory.

Many teachers believe, however, that requiring a student to write spelling corrections several times each is a waste of time because it does not result in any long-term retention of those words. They are wrong in this belief because, under certain conditions, the repeated writing of a correct word can be helpful in facilitating its storage in long-term memory (Schlagal, 2002). The conditions are:

- The student must really *want* to master the spelling of that word (i.e., is highly motivated to attend to the task with that goal in mind).
- Writing of the target word should not be repeated more than three times.
- Only a few words (no more than three) are treated this way in any one session.

Fonetik Spelling

The compensatory approach devised by Jackson (1994) acknowledges that poor spellers will probably not suddenly become good spellers and therefore they need to be taught ways to cope with their difficulties. The aim of his program *Fonetik Spelling* is to help these students produce better phonic approximations of the words they want to use, so that they can enter the words into an electronic dictionary or hand-held spell-checker and receive feedback in the form of the correct spelling. The underlying principle of the approach is that when an irregular and difficult word is written phonetically, it is at least understandable to a human reader and to a spell-checker. Spelling a word 'as it sounds' is therefore preferable to either not attempting the word at all or producing a bizarre spelling that cannot be interpreted.

In order to benefit from the program, the students are first given instruction and practice in breaking words into syllables. They are taught also that every syllable contains a vowel sound, and they are instructed in letter–sound relationships for the five short vowels (a, e, i, o, u). Jackson et al. (2003, p. 25) state: 'The key to moving from an undecipherable to a decipherable attempt to spell depends on the ability of the students to spell each and every syllable of a word in phonetic "chunks" and to ensure that vowel sounds are correctly represented.' When a target word has been analysed into its phonetic components it is entered into a spell-checker or electronic dictionary (e.g., the Franklin *TMQ-200 Electronic Dictionary*). Since there is often more than one correct way to render a word phonetically, it may be necessary sometimes to try a different vowel if the dictionary does not yield a feasible response on first entry. The students are taught appropriate strategies for dealing with this issue.

The *Fonetik Spelling* approach is intended for use with upper primary and secondary students with severe spelling difficulties. There is evidence to indicate that it is effective in improving the spelling skills of these older students, and these gains become evident after only a few periods of instruction (Jackson et al., 2003). It is probable that the need to think carefully of the letter-to-sound correspondences required to produce an accurate spelling (or a near approximation) improves a student's word-analysis ability in a way that will generalise. *Fonetik Spelling* may also increase students' confidence by giving them a self-help system to reduce their spelling problem.

Simultaneous Oral Spelling

The strategy Simultaneous Oral Spelling (SOS) can be used when first learning the correct spelling of a difficult word and is applicable across a wide age range, including secondary and tertiary education settings. The names of the letters are used rather than their phonetic sounds, so this avoids embarrassment for older learners. As with look-say-cover-write-check strategy, SOS is mainly of benefit when trying to learn or correct the spelling of irregular and complex words. This simple strategy was developed by Gillingham and Stillman in the 1960s and has been found useful in individual remedial tuition (e.g., Weeks et al., 2002).

The steps in the SOS strategy are as follows:

- Select the word you wish to learn.
- Look at it carefully and ask the tutor or teacher to pronounce the word clearly.
- Pronounce the word accurately yourself.
- Say each syllable (in a polysyllabic word).
- Name the letters in sequence, and then say the word, e.g. *w-o-r-l-d = world*.
- Repeat the letter-naming step.
- Write the word, naming each letter as it is written.

- Check and say the word.
- Write the word again from memory.

Visualisation

Visual perception and visual memory both play important roles in spelling performance, but not all individuals appear to use visual imagery to the same extent when processing information. Strategies such as look-say-cover-write-check clearly aim to strengthen visual imagery and to help with the long-term storage of correct spelling patterns. Other methods too place a premium upon visualisation. For example, in a study reported by Butyniec-Thomas and Woloshyn (1997), students in Grade 3 were trained to create visual images of target words (20 minutes of imagery training and practice daily for one week). The training involved teaching students to close their eyes and imagine they were typing the word or painting the word on a screen or chalkboard. The strategy was modelled, its value discussed, practice was given and daily review provided. They compared three groups: one received explicit strategy training alone (words not in context); one received explicit strategy training using words from whole-language contexts; and the third group engaged in whole-language writing activities without strategy training. The 'strategy training plus whole language' group produced the superior results. The least effective approach was whole language with no explicit instruction.

Some techniques borrowed from the field of neuro-linguistic programming (NLP) are also believed to be applicable for strengthening visualisation skills for weak spellers, although research findings are not conclusive (Brooks et al., 2002; Dilts, 1997). NLP is a form of psychotherapy developed in the 1970s. Some of its practices are interesting but research data to date has not given great support to the overall approach.

In NLP it is believed that one's inner language can be used to focus and control mental processes. For example, using self-regulating inner speech can help an individual adopt the most effective method for learning or recalling a word. The approach used by Dilts (1997) instructs learners to tell themselves to look at a new word carefully, then *move the eyes up and to the left* in order to visualise that word in the mind's eye. NLP practitioners believe that, for right-handed people, visualisation and recall takes place in that field. The technique may be effective in this case because it causes the individual to take a much more active role in the visualisation process.

Multisensory method

Tracing a finger over a word that is to be learned while saying the word and attending to the letter sequence is a long-established method in remedial teaching. The approach is often referred to as VAK (visual, auditory, kinaesthetic) and is often used in conjunction with other strategies, such as look-say-cover-write-check (e.g., Brooks et al., 2002; Bryan, 2003; Lee, 2001). It can be argued that a multisensory approach, using several channels of input, helps with assimilation and storage of a word pattern because it causes a learner to focus attention intently on the learning task. It is obviously easier to apply a VAK approach with younger students, but in a one-to-one remedial situation it is still a viable proposition with older students.

Peer support

One of the ways to relieve demands on teachers' time and attention in addressing students' individual learning needs is to make positive use of the students themselves in a teaching and tutoring role. Organisational options such as partner spelling and class-wide peer tutoring have proved to be useful in the domain of writing and spelling (Keller, 2002; McDonnell et al., 2004; Watkins & Hunter-Carsch, 1995). In this context, students work in pairs, either matched by ability or with a better speller assisting a less proficient speller. Tutoring sessions occur for about 10 to 20 minutes several times a week. Students are first instructed by the teacher in how to help each other learn the spelling of target words (Buschman, 2003). For additional details on training students for tutoring, see the links below.

LINKS TO MORE ON HELPING WEAKER SPELLERS

- For interesting information about the aspects of English that cause many of the difficulties with spelling, see Bell, M. (2007). *English spelling*. Retrieved January 4, 2008 from: http://englishspellingproblems.co.uk/index.html

- A full description of the NLP spelling approach (Dilts, 1997) *The NLP spelling strategy* can be found online at: http://www.nlpu.com/Articles/artic10.htm
- For practical hints for multisensory approaches to spelling, see: http://www.resourceroom.net/readspell/index.asp and http://www.bdainternationalconference.org/2001/presentations/thu_s5_a_4.htm
- For practical hints for peer tutoring and partner spelling, see: http://www.lehigh.edu/projectreach/teachers/peer_tutoring/peer_tutoring_open.htm and http://makeadifference.etsu.edu/Strategypages/peertutorspell.htm
- Practical advice for teaching children with learning difficulties is offered at: http://www.csusm.edu/Quiocho/sp.students.htm

seven

Assessing spelling skills and strategies

KEY ISSUES

- Effective teaching of spelling requires that teachers determine precisely the knowledge, skills and strategies already possessed by their students.
- Assessment of students' spelling provides an indication of their progress over time and of the effectiveness of the spelling instruction they receive.
- Some forms of assessment are related directly to the expected attainment targets and performance outcomes specified in curriculum guidelines.
- Other forms of assessment are of a diagnostic nature, used to determine the spelling strengths and weakness in individual students.
- Assessment must lead to action in terms of effective teaching and intervention.

One of the changes in classroom practice that occurred as a result of the introduction of the whole-language approach to literacy was that the routine formal testing of spelling fell out of favour in many schools. It was believed that students' spelling ability should only be appraised within the context of their daily writing. As a consequence, teachers attempted (with varying degrees of success) to address each student's spelling ability and instructional needs individually, by giving feedback on his or her writing and encouraging invented spelling. This individual form of assessment is very valuable, but if used alone it is totally inadequate as a method of evaluating the spelling development and standards within a whole class and across schools.

This chapter provides a brief overview of the purposes of assessment in spelling, the forms of assessment that are available to teachers and the educational uses that can be made of data collected from the assessment of students' spelling.

Purposes of assessment

Assessment of students' spelling serves several purposes, the principal purpose being to determine students' developmental levels and instructional needs. By analysing a student's errors on a well-constructed spelling assessment, teachers can pinpoint the student's level of spelling knowledge and can identify the types of words that are most appropriate for spelling study (Bissaker & Westwood, 2006; Templeton, 2003). In the case of weaker spellers, assessment may serve a more diagnostic function by identifying any specific weaknesses and misconceptions these students may have that need to be remedied. In other words, regular assessment of students' spelling skills is useful if it leads to positive action on the part of the teacher.

Ongoing assessment to guide instruction is usually termed 'formative' to differentiate it from 'summative' assessment that occurs much less frequently to evaluate students' learning at the end of a course of study or unit of work. Summative assessment is based on the stated learning objectives for that course.

Summative assessment is often linked to established 'benchmarks' and to 'outcome indicators' in such documents as *English: A curriculum profile for Australian Schools* (Curriculum Corporation, 1994), *Literacy: Professional elaboration* (Curriculum Corporation, 1998) and the *First steps: Spelling developmental continuum* (Education Department of Western Australia, 1994; 2004). These documents provide reasonably clear descriptions of specific knowledge, skills and strategies a student demonstrates in his or her writing at different stages of development.

A different form of assessment is represented in norm-referenced standardised testing, such as the various 'basic skills tests' carried out in many states, and in published test material. This form of assessment is important because it allows researchers and administrators to detect any changes in the general standard of spelling in schools over a period of years (e.g., Westwood & Bissaker, 2005). It also gives a teacher an indication of how children in his or her class compare with the established standard that applies generally to that age group.

Methods of assessment

Information on students' spelling skills and strategies can be obtained by using any of the following assessment procedures:

- observation
- analysis of work samples
- individual interview and discussion with a student
- formal and informal testing.

Observation

The most natural way to appraise students' spelling ability is to observe them as they write and as they attempt to use words that are a little beyond their current level of ability. Information gleaned from informal observation needs to be supplemented later with information from other sources such as work samples and test results.

Teachers should observe students in a systematic way, for example by focusing on the following points:

- Is the student confident or hesitant when writing?
- How willing is the student to take risks and attempt difficult words?
- What does the student do when faced with spelling a difficult word?
- Does the student check his or her spelling and self-correct where necessary?
- Does the student appear to have a core spelling vocabulary of the most commonly used words?

Some students need very close and regular monitoring by the teacher, others require much less. Relevant observations of specific weaknesses, gaps in learning and misconceptions need to be noted and, where necessary, translated into teaching objectives for individual students.

Work samples

Teachers can gain insight into students' spelling ability from examination of samples of their unaided writing. For example, it is possible to judge the approximate stage of development a student has reached, the knowledge he or she is relying on most when spelling difficult words, and the extent to which he or she is checking and self-correcting (Jenkins & Dix, 2004). It is also easy to observe the student's accuracy or difficulty when spelling common but important everyday words. Samples can be taken from students' exercise books, test papers and language arts portfolios (Fiderer, 1998).

Howell et al. (1993) suggest that when assessing errors teachers should be on the look-out for those that may actually reflect incorrect, careless or regional speech patterns; for example, word endings may often be omitted. They recommend checking the student's ability to pronounce a misspelled word correctly before attempting remediation.

Error analysis

In the case of the weakest spellers, it is worth looking closely at the errors they have made in order to detect what they may need to be taught (Apel & Masterson, 2001). For example:

- Are they depending too much on phonic translation, so that irregular words are written as if they are phonetically regular (e.g. *rsk* for *ask*; *werc* for *work*)?
- Are they omitting letters or syllables from multisyllabic words (e.g. *rember* for *remember*; *compter* for *computer*)?
- Are they making errors when double letters are required (e.g. *litle* for *little*; *swiming* for *swimming*)?
- Are they transposing letters (e.g. *aminal* for *animal*)?
- Are they substituting a consonant or consonant blend (e.g. *glass* for *class*; *trive* for *drive*)?
- Are they having particular difficulty with complex vowel units (e.g. *waet* for *wait*; *heit* for *heat*)?

As an example, the following list shows errors made by a secondary school student with spelling difficulties (age: 16 years 2 months) (Bissaker & Westwood, 2006). The student scored a total of 36 words correct on the South Australian spelling test, but most students of this age can spell between 53 and 64 words correctly (average 58). A score of 36 equates with typical spelling performance of a 9-year-old student.

Item	Error	(Target word)	Item	Error	(Target word)
28	fary	(fare)	45	lafter	(laughter)
32	trit	(tight)	46	fortty	(thoughtful)
33	cryed	(cried)	47	incorge	(encourage)
34	nune	(none)	48	efeshent	(efficient)
40	unell	(unusual)	49	prpicesice	(purpose)
41	quatly	(quality)	50	coreise	(curious)
42	funnter	(furniture)	55	naver	(neighbour)
44	fachen	(fashion)	57	assment	(assessment)

This student is performing well below the average standard for his age in spelling but can spell a corpus of simple regular and irregular words (as reflected in the correct responses to the simpler one- and two-syllable words in items 1 to 30 in the test). This suggests that he possesses at least adequate basic phonic knowledge. However, the student has difficulty applying phonic analysis to words such as *unusual, quality* and *furniture*, and his written attempt at such words does not produce a reasonable phonetic alternative. Some of the three- or four-syllable words are reduced to only two syllables; for example, *furniture* becomes *funnter* and *assessment* becomes *assment*). The starting point for intervention with this student should be practising orally the segmentation of multisyllabic spoken words into syllables, followed by the careful writing and checking of those words. Errors that arise in the student's written work across all school subjects can provide a starting point for such word study. It would also be useful to spend time reviewing some common orthographic units that occur across many words, for example, *–ence, –ally, –tion*. For intensive remediation of this type with an adolescent student, it is necessary to conduct regular one-to-one tutorials, rather than to attempt such assistance within a whole-class situation.

Appropriate remediation methods for specific types of spelling error are described clearly in the book *Spelling recovery* (Roberts, 2001). This book also contains useful lists of the most commonly used words and frequent spelling demons.

Testing

It is only worth using any forms of testing if doing so will yield information that can be applied to the improvement of a teaching program, or to provide information for official purposes. Testing can be regarded as either 'formal', as in the case of published tests, basic skills tests and annual examinations, or 'informal' as represented by teacher-made tests and the weekly 'quick quiz'. For the purposes of this brief overview of testing, reference will be made only to the more informal types of testing. Coverage of other forms of assessment can be found in Westwood (2005).

Two types of informal test can be of value in adding information to that obtained from direct observation and work sample analysis. These forms of test are:

- curriculum-based tests (also known as 'outcomes-based measures')
- diagnostic tests.

Curriculum-based tests

Curriculum-based tests are devised by the teacher and contain words that have been the focus of study during the preceding week. They might be thematic words related to some general classroom topic, or they might be a group of words studied to establish understanding of certain rules or orthographic units. The purpose of the testing is to determine whether the students have mastered and retained the taught knowledge or whether revision and re-teaching are necessary. These teacher-made tests can be regarded as 'check-ups' and they form one important part of the ongoing evaluation of students' learning (Jones, 2001).

Diagnostic tests

Diagnostic tests help to identify the specific needs of students with spelling difficulties. While some diagnostic information can be obtained from curriculum-based tests and from students' own written work, it is often helpful to have lists of words that allow a teacher to assess in more detail a student's grasp of particular spelling patterns, rules and conventions.

When applying diagnostic spelling tests, the teacher aims to discover in detail what spelling knowledge, skills and strategies the student can already apply, and to detect any gaps, weaknesses or misunderstandings in the student's current repertoire of skills and strategies.

Some of the material in the Appendices can be used for informal diagnostic purposes, but teachers are encouraged to devise their own informal tests along similar lines.

Interview and discussion with a student

Perhaps the most productive way of assessing spelling ability involves sitting down with a student and working through some of his or her errors, or proofreading a prepared passage that has some errors. Almost all the information teachers need to obtain concerning a student's existing knowledge, skills and strategies in spelling can be obtained by talking with the student about his or her insights into the processes of spelling, and watching the student in action while writing.

The teacher and student together can proofread some written work and the teacher can observe the student's skills and can ask for an explanation of the strategies he or she is applying. The student can be asked such questions as:

- When you need to learn the spelling of some words, how do you try to learn them?
- When you are writing, what do you do if you are not quite sure how to spell a word?
- What else could you do?
- How would you break up or sound out this word?
- What do you do if you write a word and it doesn't look right?
- How might you check this word? Where could you find the correct spelling?

The teacher has an opportunity during the interview to provide some on-the-spot instruction; for example, demonstrating an effective way of learning a target word, or checking a word with a hand-held spell-checker. The student is then asked to demonstrate and explain the procedure back to the teacher and apply it to some new examples. This form of *dynamic* assessment indicates to the teacher the student's ability to benefit immediately from instruction and feedback.

Self-assessment

Independent spellers are able to monitor the accuracy of their own spelling, and they tend to do this at all times. One of the aims for teaching spelling to all students is to move them in this direction. Loeffler (2005) describes a simple classroom method that encourages students with spelling difficulties to self-assess their spelling and to place a circle around any words they think may be incorrect as they write. When they finish the writing they go back and apply some self-checking strategies to these words, such as sounding out the phonemes, checking the vowel sounds in each syllable, checking beginning and final sounds, and having another go until the word looks and sounds right. They can also use other self-help methods such as asking a friend, using a spell-checker or a dictionary. Loeffler argues that this method helps students develop a system that can operate effectively every time they have to write.

All students can be encouraged to identify their own specific needs for instruction and to set themselves some agreed goals for the coming week. They may identify particular words that always seem to be giving them problems, and these words can be studied with the teacher's guidance and transferred to a personal list of 'spelling demons' to be kept in the back of the students' exercise books. Self-assessment and self-help of this type leads to greater independence and control.

Additional resources

Teachers requiring additional information on assessment and evaluation in spelling are referred to the *Manual for testing and teaching English spelling* by Jamieson and Jamieson (2003); *Assessment and instruction of reading and writing: An interactive approach* by Lipson and Wixson (2003); *Word journeys* by Ganske (2000); and a paper by Ganske (1999) in the journal *Educational Assessment*, 6. See references for details.

LINKS TO MORE ON ASSESSMENT

> A spelling assessment devised by University of New South Wales Assessment Centre (2006) explores spellers' use of (a) visual knowledge; (b) phonological knowledge; (c) morphological knowledge; and (d) etymological knowledge. The assessment framework is available online at: http://www.eaa.unsw.edu.au/pdf/ICAS_SpellingAF.pdf

>

- *Elementary spelling inventory* with 25 words analysed for phonic units. Available online at: http://teams.lacoe.edu/documentation/classrooms/patti/k-1/teacher/assessment/spelling.html
- *Self-assessment on spelling.* Includes error analysis, adding suffixes, consonant doubling. Available online at: http://www.phon.ucl.ac.uk/home/dick/tta/spelling/assess.htm#sindy
- *Developmental spelling assessment.* Based on Ganske's approach. Available online at: http://www.databdirect.com/Sample/EarlyReadingIntervention/2AssessmentTools.pdf
- *Spelling assessment* (Newman, 2007) with word lists covering a wide range of word forms. Available online at: http://www.lupinworks.com/os/spelling/assess.html
- Information regarding the *International English Spelling Assessment* is available online at: http://ieera.org/assessment/Spelling_Assessment.htm

Appendix 1

A core list of priority words

These words are among the most frequently used in students' writing, and all students should master their correct spelling. Some words here represent simple sound-to-letter translations but other are phonetically irregular and need to be mastered by visual methods and repeated writing.

a	but	her	more	see	to
about	by	him	mother	she	two
after	can	his	my	should	up
all	could	how	new	so	very
also	did	I	no	some	was
an	do	if	not	such	way
and	down	in	now	than	we
any	father	into	of	that	well
are	first	is	on	the	went
as	for	it	one	their	were
at	friend	its	only	them	what
back	from	just	or	then	when
be	get	know	other	there	which
because	go	like	our	these	who
been	good	little	out	they	will
being	got	made	over	think	with
between	had	make	people	this	would
big	has	many	playing	those	years
brother	have	may	said	three	you
bus	he	me	school	time	your

Appendix 2

Some predictable spelling patterns

The words here may be used for assessment of a student's ability to spell words that are phonetically regular. The list also provides an opportunity to examine the student's knowledge of a selection of consonant blends and digraphs used in the initial and final position. The final two words in each column require knowledge of syllable units.

at	if	on	up	wet
bag	rod	fin	bus	men
chop	plot	ship	trap	step
flag	swim	glad	drop	slug
must	risk	silk	send	lamp
fact	help	sift	luck	song
scrap	string	split	think	shack
winter	person	driving	action	beside
freedom	latest	project	chapter	remember

Some less predictable words

the	ask	are	any	does
said	sure	was	they	come
tough	work	master	half	lawn
laugh	wander	glove	women	where
world	juice	build	business	yacht

Appendix 3

Simple word building

Students can be asked to think of as many words as possible that can be constructed from each of these orthographic units:

–amp	–ump	–and	–end	–ast	–est	–ist
–ust	–ank	–ink	–all	–ill	–ull	–ang
–ant	–ent	–int	–unt	–old	–alk	–ilk
–elt	–ilt	–atch	–itch	–unch	–uch	–act
–ift	–ong	–orm	–orn	–ulk	–umb	–oss
–ar	–ay	–ea	–ey	–ure	–er	–ow
–dge	–tch	–eer	–igh	–ight		

Other useful orthographic units for word building

–ight	–ough	–ought	–aught	–dge	–ance	–ence	
–ange	–ose	–are	–tion	–ttle	–ddle	–tter	–bble
–cket	–ckle	–stle	–able	–ture	–ssion	–ible	–ious
–ent	–tial	–cial	–erve	–ieve	–tor	–tain	–ally

Appendix 4

Word families: two examples

Studying word families based on rhyming words helps students recognise common sequences of letters (orthographic units) that are shared by many words. For example, a typical word family can be constructed using the orthographic unit /–ack/.

back	lack	sack	stack
black	pack	slack	tack
hack	quack	smack	track
jack	rack	snack	rack

A word family based on a base word, suffixes and derivations

work	worker	worked	working
workable	workbench	workhorse	workshop
workshy	workmanship		

Appendix 5

Word sorts: an example

Each word is written on a separate card. Students are asked to find similarities and differences between the words and to generate some more words illustrating the similarities. At the end of the activity, the cards are given to one student who then dictates the words for the other students to write.

each	match	reach	batch	latch	ditch
beach	peach	patch	watch	pitch	stitch
catch	twitch	witch	hatch	teach	

References

Alber, S., & Walshe, S. (2004). When to self-correct spelling words. *Journal of Behavioral Education, 13, 1,* 51–66.

Albuera Street Primary School (Hobart). (2004). *Spelling: Scope and sequence.* Department of Education, Tasmania. Retrieved December 30, 2007 from: http://www.ltag.education.tas.gov.au/focus/beingliterate/Albueraspelling.pdf

Andrews, S., & Scarratt, D. (1996). What comes after phonological awareness? Using lexical experts to investigate orthographic processes in reading. *Australian Journal of Psychology, 48, 3,* 141–148.

Apel, K., & Masterson, J. J. (2001). Theory-guided spelling assessment and intervention: A case study. *Language, Speech and Hearing Services in Schools, 32,* 182–195.

Ashton, T. M. (1999). Spell checking: Making writing meaningful in the inclusive classroom. *Teaching Exceptional Children, 32, 2,* 24–27.

Ball, E. W., & Blachman, B. A. (1991). Does phonemic awareness training in kindergarten make a difference in early word recognition and developmental spelling? *Reading Research Quarterly, 27,* 49–66.

Barone, D. (1992). Whatever happened to spelling? *Reading Psychology, 13, 1,* 1–17.

Bean, W. (1998). Spelling across the grades. In J. Coombs (Ed.), *Getting started: Ideas for the literacy teacher.* Newtown, NSW: Primary English Teaching Association.

Berninger, V. W., Abbott, R. D., Whitaker, D., Sylvester, L., & Nolen, S. B. (1995). Integrating low and high-level skills in instructional protocols for writing disabilities. *Learning Disabilities Quarterly, 18, 4,* 293–309.

Berninger, V. W., Vaughn, K., Abbott, R. D., Brooks, A., Abbott, S., & Rogan, L. (1998). Early intervention for spelling problems: Teaching functional spelling units of varying size with a multiple connections framework. *Journal of Educational Psychology, 90,* 587–605.

Bhattacharya, A. (2006). Syllable-based reading strategy for mastery of scientific information. *Remedial and Special Education 27, 2,* 116–23.

Bhattacharya, A., & Ehri, L. (2004). Graphosyllabic analysis helps adolescent struggling readers read and spell words. *Journal of Learning Disabilities, 37, 4,* 331–348.

Bissaker, K., & Westwood, P. (2006). Diagnostic uses of the South Australian Spelling Test. *Australian Journal of Learning Disabilities, 11, 1,* 25–3.

Blachman, B. A., Ball, E. W., Black, R., & Tangel, D. M. (2000). *Road to the code: A phonological awareness program for young children.* Baltimore, MD: Brookes.

Board of Studies New South Wales. (2007). *Supporting your child's learning: Spelling K–6.* Retrieved December 21, 2007 from: http://www.boardofstudies.nsw.edu.au/parents/kspelling.html

Bos, C., Mather, N., Dickson, S., Podhajski, B., & Chard, D. (2001). Perceptions and knowledge of preservice and inservice educators about early reading instruction. *Annals of Dyslexia, 51,* 97–120.

Bower, B. (2001). Learning in waves: Kids sail through many strategies to reach isles of knowledge. *Science News, 159, 11,* 172–174.

Bradley, L. (1983). The organisation of visual, phonological, and motor strategies in learning to read and spell. In U. Kirk (Ed.), *Neuropsychology of language, reading and spelling.* New York: Academic Press.

Bryan, T. (2003). A kinaesthetic approach to spelling and handwriting. *Primary & Middle Years Educator, 1, 3,* 14–17.

Bryant, P., & Bradley, L. (1983). Categorising sounds and learning to read: A causal connection. *Nature, 30,* 419–421.

Bryant, P., & Bradley, L. (1985). *Children's reading problems.* Oxford: Blackwell.

Buschman, L. (2003). Buddies aren't just for reading: They're for spelling too. *The Reading Teacher, 56, 8,* 747–752.

Butyniec-Thomas, J., & Woloshyn, V. E. (1997). The effects of explicit strategy and whole-language instruction on students' spelling ability. *Journal of Experimental Education, 65, 4,* 293–302.

Canado, M. L. (2006). The effects of explicit spelling instruction in the Spanish EFL classroom: Diagnosis, development and durability. *Language Awareness, 15, 1,* 20–37.

Cardoso-Martins, C., Correa, M. F., Lemos, L. S., & Napoleao, R. (2006). Is there a syllabic stage in spelling development? Evidence from Portuguese-speaking children. *Journal of Educational Psychology, 98, 3,* 628–641.

Carmichael, R., & Hempenstall, K. (2006). Building upon sound foundations. *Australian Journal of Learning Disabilities, 11, 1,* 3–16.

Cates, G. L., Dunne, M., Erkfritz, K. N., Kivisto, A., Lee, N., & Wierzbieki, J. (2007). Differential effects of two spelling procedures on acquisition, maintenance and adaptation to reading. *Journal of Behavioral Education, 16, 1,* 71–81.

Cavey, D. W. (2000). *Dysgraphia: Why Johnny can't write* (3rd ed.). Austin, TX: ProEd.

Chandler, K. (2000). What I wish I'd known about teaching spelling. *English Journal: High School Edition, 89, 6,* 87–95.

Chliounaki, K., & Bryant, P. (2007). How children learn about morphological spelling rules. *Child Development, 78, 4*, 1360–1373.

Clarke-Klein, S. M. (1994). Expressive phonological deficiencies: Impact on spelling development. *Topics in Language Disorders, 14, 2*, 40–55.

Coleman-Martin, M. B., & Heller, K. W. (2004). Using a modified constant prompt-delay procedure to teach spelling to students with physical disabilities. *Journal of Applied Behaviour Analysis, 37, 4*, 469–480.

Commonwealth of Australia. (1997). *Literacy standards in Australia.* Canberra: Australian Government Publishing Service.

Cripps, C. (1990). Teaching joined writing to children on school entry as an agent for catching spelling. *Australian Journal of Remedial Education, 22, 3*, 13–15.

Critten, S., Pine, K., & Steffler, D. (2007). Spelling development in young children: A case of representational redescription? *Journal of Educational Psychology, 99, 1*, 207–220.

Curriculum Corporation. (1994). *English: A curriculum profile for Australian schools.* Melbourne: Curriculum Corporation.

Curriculum Corporation. (1998). *Literacy: Professional elaboration.* Melbourne: Curriculum Corporation.

Curriculum Corporation. (2000). *Benchmarks for literacy and numeracy.* Melbourne: Curriculum Corporation.

Dahl, K. & Associates (2003). Connecting developmental word study with classroom writing: Children's descriptions of spelling strategies. *The Reading Teacher, 57, 4*, 310–319.

Darch, C., Kim, S., Johnson, J. H., & James, J. (2000). The strategic spelling skills of students with learning disabilities: The results of two studies. *Journal of Instructional Psychology, 27, 1*, 15–27.

Davies, A., & Ritchie, D. (2004). *Teaching Handwriting, Reading and Spelling Skills (THRASS).* Chester: THRASS (UK) Ltd.

DE (Department of Education, Tas.). (2007a). *Six spelling principles.* Retrieved December 21, 2007 from: http://wwwfp.education.tas.gov.au/english/six.htm

DE (Department of Education, Tas.). (2007b). *Spelling strategies.* Retrieved December 27, 2007 from: http://wwwfp.education.tas.gov.au/english/spellstrat.htm

Deacon, S. H., & Bryant, P. (2006). This turnip's not for turning: Children's morphological awareness and their use of root morphemes in spelling. *British Journal of Developmental Psychology, 24*, 567–575.

DECS (SA) (Department for Education and Children's Services, South Australia). (1997). *Spelling: From beginnings to independence.* Adelaide: DECS.

Delattre, M., Bonin, P., & Barry, C. (2006). Written spelling to dictation: Sound-to-spelling regularity affects both writing latencies and durations. *Journal of Experimental Psychology: Learning, Memory and Cognition, 32, 6*, 1330–1340.

DES (Department of Education and Skills, UK). (2006). *Primary framework for literacy and mathematics*. Retrieved January 8, 2008 from: http://www.standards.dfes.gov.uk/primaryframeworks/literacy/

DET (NSW) (Department of Education and Training, NSW). (1998). *Teaching spelling K–6*. Sydney: NSW Department for Education and Training.

DfCSF (Department for Children, Schools and Families, UK). (2002). *Towards the National Curriculum for English*. The Standards Site. Retrieved January 10, 2008 from: http://www.standards.dfes.gov.uk/primary/publications/literacy/63361

DfEE (Department for Education and Employment, UK). (1998). *The National Literacy Strategy*. London: DfEE.

Dickinson, P. (2003). Whole class interactive teaching. *SET Research for Teachers*, 1, 18–21. Wellington: New Zealand Council for Educational Research.

Dilts, R. (1997). *The NLP spelling strategy*. Retrieved January 9, 2008 from: http://www.nlpu.com/Articles/article10.htm

Dixon, R. C. (1991). The application of sameness analysis to spelling. *Journal of Learning Disabilities, 24*, 5, 285–291.

Dixon, R., & Engelmann, S. (1976). *Spelling through morphographs*. Sydney: SRA/McGraw-Hill.

DuBois, K., Erickson, K., & Jacobs. M. (2007). *Improving spelling of high frequency words for transfer in written work: an action research project*. Chicago, IL: St Xavier University and Pearson Achievement Solutions. ERIC Document ED 496700.

Education Department of Western Australia (1994; 2004). *First steps: Spelling developmental continuum*. Melbourne: Longman Cheshire.

Egan, J., & van Gorder, J. (1998). Spelling back on the agenda. *Primary Educator, 4*, 2, 1–3.

Ehri, L. (1997). Learning to read and learning to spell are one and the same, almost. In C. A. Perfetti, L., Rieben, & M. Fayol (Eds.), *Learning to spell: Research, theory and practice across languages* (pp. 237–269). Mahwah, NJ: Erlbaum.

Ehri, L., & Wilce, L. (1985). Movement into reading: Is the first stage of printed word learning visual or phonetic? *Reading Research Quarterly, 20*, 163–179.

Elbro, C., & Arnbak, E. (1996). The role of morpheme recognition and morphological awareness in dyslexia. *Annals of Dyslexia, 46*, 209–240.

Eldredge, J. L. (2005). *Teach decoding: Why and how* (2nd ed.). Upper Saddle River, NJ: Pearson-Merrill-Prentice Hall.

Ellis, L. A. (2005) *Balancing approaches: Revisiting the educational psychology research on teaching students with learning difficulties*. Melbourne: Australian Council for Educational Research.

Ferrari, J. (2006). Singapore kids spell better than Aussies. *The Australian*, 27 July 2006, n.p.

Fiderer, A. (1998). Assessing literacy levels in your classroom. *Classroom, 98, 2*, 18–19.

Foorman, B. R., Schatschneider, C., Eakin, M. N., Fletcher, J. M., Moats, L., & Francis, D. J. (2006). The impact of instructional practices in Grades 1 and 2 on reading and spelling achievement in poverty schools. *Contemporary Educational Psychology, 31, 1*, 1–29.

Frank, M. (2007). The importance of word study. *NetNews, 7, 3*, 1–4. ERIC document ED498939.

Fresch, M. J. (2007). Teachers' concerns about spelling instruction: A national survey. *Reading Psychology, 28, 4*, 301–330.

Fulk, B. M. (1996). The effects of combined strategy and attribution training on LD adolescents' spelling performance. *Exceptionality, 6, 1*, 13–27.

Fulk, B. M. (1997). Think while you spell: A cognitive motivational approach to spelling instruction. *Teaching Exceptional Children, 29, 4*, 70–71.

Fulk, B. M., & Stormont-Spurgin, M. (1995). Spelling interventions for students with disabilities: A review. *Journal of Special Education, 28*, 488–513.

Ganske, K. (1999). The developmental spelling analysis: A measure of orthographic knowledge. *Educational Assessment, 6*, 41–70.

Ganske, K. (2000). *Word journeys*. New York: Guilford.

Gentry, J. R. (2001). Five myths about spelling. *Instructor, 111, 3*, 31–33.

Gentry, J. R. (2004). *The science of spelling*. Portsmouth, NH: Heinemann.

Gillingham, A., & Stillman, B. (1960). *Remedial teaching for children with specific disability in reading, spelling and penmanship*. Cambridge, MA: Educators Publishing Service.

Glass, L., Peist, L., & Pike, B. (2000). *Read! Read! Read! Training effective reading partners*. Thousand Oaks, CA: Corwin Press.

Gordon, J., Vaughn, S. & Schumm, J. S. (1993). Spelling interventions: A review of literature and implications for instruction for students with learning disabilities. *Learning Disabilities Research and Practice, 8*, 175–181.

Graham, S. (2000). Should the natural learning approach replace spelling instruction? *Journal of Educational Psychology, 92, 2*, 235–247.

Graham, S., Harris, K., & Chorzempa, B. F. (2002). Contribution of spelling instruction to the spelling, writing and reading of poor spellers. *Journal of Educational Psychology, 94, 4*, 669–686.

Graham, S., Harris, K., & Loynachan, C. (1994). The spelling for writing list. *Journal of Learning Disabilities, 27, 4*, 210–214.

Graham, S., Harris, K., & Loynachan, C. (1996). The Directed Spelling Thinking Activity: Application with high-frequency words. *Learning Disabilities: Research and Practice, 11, 1*, 34–40.

Grainger, J. (1997). *Children's behaviour, attention and reading problems*. Melbourne: Australian Council for Educational Research.

Gregg, N., & Mather, N. (2002). School is fun at recess: Informal analyses of written language for students with learning disabilities. *Journal of Learning Disabilities 35, 1,* 7–22.

Griffiths, R. (2004). *Spelling in the curriculum: One hundred years of pain and confusion.* Wellington: Ministry of Education, New Zealand. Retrieved December 19, 2007 from: http://english.unitecnology.ac.nz/resources/resources/spelling.html

Hammond, L. (2004). Getting the right balance: Effective classroom spelling instruction. *Australian Journal of Learning Disabilities, 9,* 3, 11–18.

Hannam, R., Fraser, H., & Byrne, B. (2007). The sbelling of sdops: Preliterate children's spelling of stops after /s/. *Reading and Writing: An Interdisciplinary Journal, 20, 4,* 399–412.

Hardman, F., Smith, F, Mroz, M., & Wall, K. (2003). *Interactive whole class teaching in the national literacy and numeracy strategies.* Paper presented at the British Educational Research Association Conference, Edinburgh, 1–13 September 2005. Retrieved January 1, 2008 from: http://www.leeds.ac.uk/educol/documents/00003267

Harrison, G. L. (2005). The spelling strategies of students with varying graphophonemic skills: implications for instruction and intervention. *Exceptionality Education Canada, 15, 3,* 57–76.

Heilman, A. W. (2006). *Phonics in proper perspective* (10th ed.). Upper Saddle River, NJ: Merrill-Prentice Hall.

Hempenstall, K. (2002). Phonological processing and phonics: Towards an understanding of their relationship to each other and to reading development. *Australian Journal of Learning Disabilities, 7, 1,* 4–28.

Henderson, E. H., & Beers, J. (Eds.) (1980). *Developmental and cognitive aspects of learning to spell: A reflection of word knowledge.* Newark, DE: International Reading Association.

Hetzroni, O. E., & Shrieber, B. (2004). Word processing as an assistive technology tool for enhancing academic outcomes for students with writing difficulties in the general classroom. *Journal of Learning Disabilities, 37, 2,* 143–154.

Hilte, M., Bos, M., & Reitsma, P. (2005). Effects of pronunciations during spelling practice in Dutch. *Written Language and Literacy, 8, 2,* 137–153.

Hilte, M., & Reitsma, P. (2006). Spelling pronunciation and visual preview both facilitate learning to spell irregular words. *Annals of Dyslexia, 56, 2,* 301–318.

Ho, C. S. H., & Bryant, P. (1997). Learning to read Chinese beyond the logographic phase. *Reading Research Quarterly, 32, 3,* 276–289.

Ho, C. S. H., Chan, D. W. O., Tsang, S. M., & Lee, S. H. (2002). The cognitive profile and multiple-deficit hypothesis in Chinese developmental dyslexia. *Developmental Psychology, 38,* 543–553.

Holmes, V. M., & Davis, C. W. (2002). Orthographic representation and spelling knowledge. *Language and Cognitive Processes, 17, 4*, 345–370.

Holmes, V. M., & Malone, N. (2004). Adult spelling strategies. *Reading and Writing: An Interdisciplinary Journal, 17*, 537–566.

House of Commons Education and Skills Committee (UK). (2005) *Teaching Children to Read*, London: HMSO.

House of Representatives Standing Committee on Employment, Education and Training (Australia). (1992). *The literacy challenge: Strategies for early intervention for literacy and learning for Australian children.* Canberra: Australian Government Publishing Service.

Hurry, J., Bryant, P. Nunes, T., & Pretzlik, U. (2005). *Teachers' awareness of morphemes.* Retrieved December 17, 2007 from: http://www.education.ox.ac.uk/uploaded/teachersawarenessofmorphemes2005_1.pdf

Invernizzi, M., Abouzeid, M., & Gill, J. T. (1994). Using students' invented spellings as a guide for spelling instruction that emphasizes word study. *Elementary School Journal, 95, 2*, 155–167.

Invernizzi, M., & Hayes, L. (2004). Developmental spelling research: A systematic imperative. *Reading Research Quarterly, 39*, 216–228.

Jackson, C. C. (1994). *The Fonetik Spelling Program.* Wellington: New Zealand Special Education Service.

Jackson, C. C., Konza, D. M., Ben-Evans, J., & Roodenrys, S. (2003). Spelling accuracy for secondary students with spelling difficulties: Using phonetic codes and technology. *Australian Journal of Learning Disabilities, 8, 1*, 23–29.

Jamieson, C., & Jamieson, J. (2003). *Manual for testing and teaching English spelling: A comprehensive and structured system for the planning and delivery of spelling intervention.* London: Whurr.

Jenkins, H. J., & Dix, S. B. (2004). The role of action research in learning support: A case study. *Special Education Perspectives, 13, 2*, 47–68.

Johnson, D. J., & Myklebust, H. R. (1967). *Learning disabilities: Educational principles and practices.* New York: Grune & Stratton.

Johnston, F. R. (1999). The timing and teaching of word families. *The Reading Teacher, 53, 1*, 64–76.

Johnston, F. R. (2001). Exploring classroom teachers' spelling practices and beliefs. *Reading Research and Instruction, 40, 2*, 143–156.

Johnston, R., & Watson, J. (2005). A seven years study of the effects of synthetic phonics teaching on reading and spelling attainment. *Insight 17*, Edinburgh: Scottish Executive Education Department.

Jones, C. J. (2001). Teacher-friendly curriculum-based assessment in spelling. *Teaching Exceptional Children, 34, 2*, 32–38.

Joseph, L. M. (2002). Facilitating word recognition and spelling using word boxes and word sort phonic procedures. *School Psychology Review, 31, 1,* 122–129.

Joseph, L. M., & McCachran, M. (2003). Comparison of a word study phonics technique between students with moderate to mild mental retardation and learning disabilities. *Education and Training in Developmental Disabilities, 38, 2,* 192–199.

Joseph, L. M., & Orlins, A. (2005). Multiple uses of a word study technique. *Reading Improvement, 42, 2,* 73–77.

Keller, C. (2002). A new twist on spelling instruction for elementary school teachers. *Intervention in School and Clinic, 38, 1,* 3–8.

Kelly, G. (2006). A check on Look-Cover-Write-Check. *Learning Difficulties Australia Bulletin, 38, 1,* 6–7.

Kelman, M. E., & Apel, K. (2004). Effects of a multiple linguistic and prescriptive approach to spelling instruction: A case study. *Communication Disorders Quarterly, 25, 2,* 56–67.

Kemp, N. (2006). Children's spelling of base, inflected and derived words: Links with morphological awareness. *Reading and Writing: An Interdisciplinary Journal, 19, 7,* 737–765.

Kervin, L. (2002). Proofreading as a strategy for spelling development. *Reading Online, 5, 10* (n.p.).

Kervin, L., & McKenzie, K. (2005). Keeping the conversation going: Creating a whole school approach to spelling. *Conference Proceedings: Pleasure, Passion, Provocation.* AATE/ALEA National Conference, 1–4 July 2005: Broadbeach, Qld. Retrieved December 16, 2007 from: http://alea.edu.au/site-content/Kervin_McKenzie.pdf

Kirkbride, S., & Wright, B. C. (2002). The role of analogy use in improving early spelling performance. *Educational and Child Psychology, 19, 4,* 91–102.

Kolodziej, N. J., & Columba, L. (2005). Invented spelling: Guidelines for parents: *Reading Improvement, 42, 4,* 212–223.

Lam, B. F. Y., & Westwood, P. (2006). Spelling and ESL learners: A strategy training approach. *Special Education Perspectives, 15, 1,* 12–24.

Lee, J. (2001). *Spelling success at last! A system for teaching adults to spell priority words so they remain in long-term memory.* Paper presented at the 5th International Conference of the British Dyslexia Association, 7 January 2002. Retrieved January 9, 2008 from: http://www.bdinternationalconference.org/2001/presentations/thu_s5_a_4.htm

Lewis, R. B., Graves, A. W., Ashton, T. M., & Kieley, C. L. (1998). Word processing tools for students with learning disabilities: A comparison of strategies to increase text entry speed. *Learning Disabilities Research and Practice, 13,* 95–108.

Lightfoot, A. (2005). *Using dictation*. British Council: Teaching English website. Retrieved January 5, 2008 from: http://www.teachingenglish.org.uk/think/methodology/dictation.shtml

Lipka, O., & Siegel, L. S. (2007). The development of reading skills in children with English as a second language. *Scientific Studies in Reading, 11, 2*, 105–131.

Lipson, M., & Wixson, K. (2003). *Assessment and instruction of reading and writing: An interactive approach*. Boston: Allyn & Bacon.

Loeffler, K. A. (2005). No more Friday spelling tests? An alternative spelling assessment for students with learning disabilities. *Teaching Exceptional Children, 37, 4*, 24–27.

Louden, W., & Rohl, M. (2006). 'Too many theories and not enough instruction': Perceptions of pre-service teacher preparation for literacy teaching in Australia. *Literacy, 40, 2*, 66–78.

Lyndon, H. (1989). I did it my way: An introduction to Old Way – New Way. *Australasian Journal of Special Education, 13*, 32–37.

Lyon, G. R., Fletcher, J. M., & Barnes, M. C. (2003). Learning disabilities. In E. J. Mash & R. A. Barkley (Eds.), *Child psychopathology* (2nd ed.) (pp. 520–586). New York: Guilford.

MacArthur, C. A., Graham, S., Haynes, J. B., & De La Paz, S. (1996). Spelling checkers and students with learning disabilities, *Journal of Special Education, 30*, 35–57.

McDonnell, J., Thorson, N., Allen, C., & Mathot-Buckner, C. (2004). The effects of partner learning during spelling for students with severe disabilities and their peers. *Journal of Behavioral Education, 10, 2*, 107–121.

McNaughton, D., Hughes, C., & Clark, K. (1994). Spelling instruction for students with learning disabilities: Implications for research and practice. *Learning Disability Quarterly, 17*, 169–185.

Manning, M., & Underbakke, C. (2005). Spelling development research necessitates the replacement of weekly word lists. *Childhood Education, 81, 4*, 236–238.

Martins, M. A., & Silva, C. (2006). The impact of invented spelling on phonemic awareness. *Learning and Instruction, 16, 1*, 41–56.

Massengill, D. (2006). Mission accomplished, it's learnable now: Voices of mature challenged spellers using a word study approach. *Journal of Adolescent and Adult Literacy, 49, 5*, 420–431.

Mastropieri, M. A., & Scruggs, T. E. (2002). *Effective instruction for special education* (3rd ed.). Austin, TX: ProEd.

Mather, N., & Goldstein, S. (2001). *Learning disabilities and challenging behaviour*. Baltimore: Brookes.

MCEETYA (Ministerial Council on Employment, Education and Youth Affairs, Australia). (1997) *The National Literacy and Numeracy Plan*. Canberra: MCEETYA.

Meehan, R., & Hammond, L. (2006). Walking the talk: Western Australian teachers' beliefs about early reading and spelling instruction and their knowledge of meta-linguistics. *Australian Journal of Learning Disabilities, 11, 1,* 17–24.

Mesmer, H. A. E & Griffith, P. L. (2006). Everybody's selling it – but just what is explicit, systematic phonics instruction? *The Reading Teacher, 59, 4,* 366–76.

Milone, M. N., Wilhide, J. A., & Wasylyk, T. M. (1983). Spelling and handwriting: Is there a relationship? *Spelling Progress Bulletin,* Summer issue, 14–16. Retrieved December 27, 2007 from: http://www.spellingsociety.org/bulletins/b83/Summer/handwriting.php

Minton, P. (2002). Using Information and Communication Technology (ICT) to help dyslexics, and others, learn to spell. *Australian Journal of Learning Disabilities, 7, 3,* 26–31.

Moats, L. C. (1994). The missing foundation in teacher education: Knowledge of the structure of spoken and written language. *Annals of Dyslexia, 44,* 81–102.

Moats, L. C. (1995). *Spelling: Development, disability and instruction.* Baltimore: York Press.

Montgomery, D. J., Karlan, G. R., & Coutinho, M. (2001). The effectiveness of word processor spell checker programs to produce target words for misspellings generated by students with learning disabilities, *Journal of Special Education Technology, 16, 2,* 27–41.

Moore, C., Evans, D., & Dowson, M. (2005). The intricate nature of phonological awareness instruction. *Special Education Perspectives 14, 1,* 37–54.

Moseley, D. (1997). Assessment of spelling and related aspects of written expression. In J. R. Beech & C. Singleton (Eds.), *The psychological assessment of reading.* London: Routledge.

National Reading Panel (US). (2000). *Teaching children to read: An evidence-based assessment of the scientific research literature on reading and its implications for reading instruction.* Washington, DC: National Institute of Child Health and Human Development.

Nichols, R. (1985). *Helping your child spell.* Earley: University of Reading.

Nies, K. A., & Belfiore, P. J. (2006). Enhancing spelling performance in students with learning disabilities. *Journal of Behavioral Education, 15, 3,* 162–169.

Noell, G. H., Connell, J. E., & Duhon, G. J. (2006). Spontaneous response generalisation during whole word instruction: Reading to spell and spelling to read. *Journal of Behavioral Education, 15, 3,* 121–130.

Notenboom, A., & Reitsma, P. (2003). Investigating the dimensions of spelling ability. *Educational and Psychological Measurement, 63, 6,* 1039–1059.

Nugent, C. (2005). *How Australian Ministers for Education were hoodwinked.* Retrieved December 30, 2007 from: http://www.literacytesting.com/documents/WordDocB.doc

Nunes, T., Bindman, M., & Bryant, P. (1997). Morphological spelling strategies: Developmental stages and processes. *Developmental Psychology, 33,* 637–649.

Nunes, T., Bryant, P., & Bindman, M. (2006). The effects of learning to spell on children's awareness of morphology. *Reading and Writing: An Interdisciplinary Journal, 19, 7,* 767–787.

Nunes, T., Bryant, P., & Olsson, J. M. (2003). Learning morphological and phonological spelling rules: An intervention study. *Scientific Studies in Reading, 7,* 273–287.

Ormrod, J. E., & Jenkins, L. (1989). Study strategies for learning spelling: Correlations with achievement and developmental changes. *Perceptual and Motor Skills, 68,* 643–650.

O'Sullivan, O. (2000). Understanding spelling. *Reading, 34, 1,* 9–16.

Padget, S. Y., Knight, D. F., & Sawyer, D. J. (1996). Tennessee meets the challenge of dyslexia. *Annals of Dyslexia, 46,* 51–72.

Peters, M. L. (1970). *Success in spelling.* Cambridge: Cambridge Institute of Education.

Peters, M. L. (1974). Teacher variables in spelling. In B. Wade & K. Wedell (Eds.), *Spelling: Task and learner.* Birmingham: University of Birmingham Press.

Peters, M. L (1985). *Spelling: Caught or taught? A new look.* London: Routledge.

Plaza, M., & Cohen, H. (2007). The contribution of phonological awareness and visual attention in early reading and spelling. *Dyslexia, 13,* 67–76.

Poulter, M. (2002). Focus on spelling. *Literacy Today, 32,* 10–11.

Pullen, P. C., Lane, H. B., Lloyd, J. W., Nowak, R., & Ryals, J. (2005). Effects of explicit instruction on decoding of struggling first grade students: A data-based case study. *Education and Treatment of Children, 28, 1,* 63–75.

QCA (Qualifications and Curriculum Authority, UK). (2007). *English in action.* Retrieved December 30, 2007 from: http://www.ncaction.org.uk?subjects/english/progress.htm

Rahbari, N., Senechal, M., & Arab-Moghaddam, N. (2007). The role of orthographic and phonological processing skills in the reading and spelling of monolingual Persian children. *Reading and Writing: An Interdisciplinary Journal, 50, 5,* 511–533.

Ralston, M., & Robinson, G. (1997). Spelling strategies and metacognitive awareness in skilled and unskilled spellers. *Australian Journal of Learning Disabilities, 2, 4,* 12–23.

Read, C. (1971). Preschool children's knowledge of English phonology. *Harvard Educational Review, 41,* 1–34.

Read, C., & Hodges, R. E. (1982). Spelling. In H. E. Mitzel, J. H. Best & W. Rabinowitz (Eds.), *Encyclopedia of Educational Research* (5th ed.). London: Collier Macmillan.

Richards, R. G. (1999). *The source book for dyslexia and dysgraphia.* East Moline, IL: Linguisystems.

Rittle-Johnson, B., & Siegler, R. S. (1999). Learning to spell: Variability, choice and change in children's strategy use. *Child Development, 70, 2,* 332–348.

Roaf, C. (1998). Slow hand: A secondary school survey of handwriting speed and legibility. *Support for Learning, 13, 1,* 39–42.

Roberts, J. (2001). *Spelling recovery: The pathway to spelling success.* Melbourne: Australian Council for Educational Research.

Rose, J. (2005). *Independent review of the teaching of early reading: Interim report.* London: Department for Education and Skills.

Rowell, C. G. (2007). Spelling woes. *Reading Horizons, 47, 4,* 336.

Santoro, L. E., Coyne, M. D., & Simmons, D. C. (2006). The reading-spelling connection: Developing and evaluating a beginning spelling intervention for children at risk of reading disability. *Learning Disabilities Research and Practice, 12, 2,* 122–133.

Savage, R. S., & Frederickson, N. (2006). Beyond phonology: What else is needed to describe the problems of below-average readers and spellers? *Journal of Learning Disabilities, 39, 5,* 399–413.

Schlagal, B. (2001). Traditional, developmental and structured language approaches to spelling: Research and recommendations. *Annals of Dyslexia, 51,* 147–176.

Schlagal, B. (2002). Classroom spelling instruction: history, research and practice. *Reading Research and Instruction, 42, 1,* 44–57.

Senechal, M., Basque, M. T., & Leclaire, T. (2006). Morphological knowledge is revealed in children's spelling accuracy and reports of spelling strategies. *Journal of Experimental Child Psychology, 95, 4,* 231–154.

Siegler, R. S. (1996). *Emerging minds: The process of change in children's thinking.* New York: Oxford University Press.

Siegler, R. S. (2000). The rebirth of children's learning. *Child Development, 71, 1,* 26–35.

Silva, C., & Alves-Martins, M. A. (2003). Relations between children's invented spelling and the development of phonological awareness. *Educational Psychology, 23, 1,* 4–16.

Sipe, L. R. (2001). Invention, convention and intervention: Invented spelling and the teacher's role. *The Reading Teacher 53, 3,* 264–273.

Spear-Swerling, L. (2006). *The importance of teaching handwriting.* Retrieved December 27, 2007 from http://www.ldonline.org/spearswerling/10521

Steffler, D. J. (2001). Implicit cognition and spelling development. *Developmental Review, 21,* 168–204.

Strattman, K., & Hodson, B. W. (2005). Variables that influence decoding and spelling in beginning readers. *Child Language Teaching and Therapy, 21, 2,* 165–190.

Teaching & Learning Research Project (2006). Are morphemes the key to spelling? *Literacy Today, 47,* 32.

Templeton, S. (2003). The spelling-meaning connection. *Voices from the Middle, 10, 3,* 56–57.

Templeton, S. (2004). Spelling and the middle school English language learner. *Voices from the Middle, 11, 4,* 48–49.

Templeton, S., & Morris, D. (1999). Questions teachers ask about spelling. *Reading Research Quarterly, 34, 1,* 102–112.

Thibodeau, G. (2002). Spellbound: Commitment to correctness. *Voices from the Middle, 9, 3,* 19–22.

Thomson, M. (1995). Evaluating teaching programs for children with specific learning difficulties. *Australian Journal of Remedial Education, 27, 1,* 20–27.

Torgerson, C. J., & Elbourne, D. (2002). A systematic review and meta-analysis of the effectiveness of information and communication technology (ICT) on the teaching of spelling. *Journal of Research in Reading, 25,* 129–143.

Treiman, R., & Kessler, B. (2006). Spelling as statistical learning: Using consonantal contexts to spell vowels. *Journal of Educational Psychology, 98, 3,* 642–652.

Treiman, R., Kessler, B., & Bourassa, D. (2001). Children's own names influence their spelling. *Applied Linguistics, 22, 4,* 555–570.

van Hell, J. G., Bosman, A. M., & Bartelings, M. C. (2003). Visual dictation improves the spelling performance of three groups of Dutch students with spelling disabilities. *Learning Disability Quarterly, 26, 4,* 239–256.

Varnhagen, C. K., Varnhagen, S., & Das, J. P. (1992). Analysis of cognitive processing and spelling errors of average and reading-disabled children. *Reading Psychology, 13, 3,* 217–239.

Vedora, J., & Stromer, R. (2007). Computer-based spelling instruction for students with developmental disabilities. *Research in Developmental Disabilities, 28, 5,* 489–505.

Verhoeven, L., & Carlisle, J. F. (2006). Morphology in word identification and spelling. *Reading & Writing: An Interdisciplinary Journal, 19, 7,* 643–650.

Vukovic, R. K., & Siegel, L. S. (2006). The double-deficit hypothesis: A comprehensive analysis of the evidence. *Journal of Learning Disabilities 39, 1,* 25–47.

Wakefield, P. (2006). Deaf children's approaches to spelling: Difficulties, strategies and teaching techniques. *Deafness and Education International, 8, 4,* 174–189.

Wallace, R. R. (2006). Characteristics of effective spelling instruction. *Reading Horizons, 46, 4,* 267–278.

Wanzek, J., Vaughn, S., Wexler, J., Swanson, E. A., Edmonds, M., & Kim, A. H. (2006). A synthesis of spelling and reading interventions and their effects on the spelling outcomes of students with LD. *Journal of Learning Disabilities, 39, 6,* 528–543.

Watkins, G., & Hunter-Carsch, M. (1995). Prompt spelling: A practical approach to paired spelling. *Support for Learning, 10, 3,* 133–137.

Weeks, S., Brooks, P., & Everatt, J. (2002). Differences in learning to spell: Relationships between cognitive profiles and learning responses to teaching methods. *Educational and Child Psychology, 19, 4,* 47–62.

Westwood, P. (1979). *Helping children with spelling difficulties.* Adelaide: Education Department of South Australia.

Westwood, P. (1994). *Spelling achievement of students in South Australian Government Schools: 1978–1993.* Report to the Minister for Education. Adelaide: Government of South Australia.

Westwood, P. (2005). *Spelling: Approaches to teaching and assessment* (2nd ed.). Melbourne: Australian Council for Educational Research.

Westwood, P. (2008). Revisiting issues in spelling instruction: A literature review 1995–2007. *Special Education Perspectives, 17, 1,* 33–48.

Westwood, P., & Bissaker, K. (2005). Trends in spelling standards, 1978–2004: A South Australian study. *The Australian Educational and Developmental Psychologist, 22, 1,* 65–76.

Wheatley, J. P. (2005). *Strategic spelling: Moving beyond word memorization in the middle grades.* Newark, DE: International Reading Association.

Wheeldon, J. (2006). Why teachers should be spellbound. *Weekend Australian,* 29 July, p. 21.

Whiting, P. R., & Chapman, E. (2000). Evaluation of a computer-based program to teach reading and spelling to students with learning difficulties. *Australian Journal of Learning Disabilities, 5, 4,* 11–17.

Wilde, S. (2004). Spelling today. *School Talk.* Urbana, IL: National Council of Teachers of English.

Williams, J. (1986). The role of phonemic analysis in reading. In J. Torgesen & B. Wong (Eds.), *Psychological and educational perspectives on learning disabilities.* Orlando: Academic Press.

Wirtz, C. L., Gardner, R., Weber, K., & Bullara, D. (1996). Using self-correction to improve the spelling performance of low-achieving third graders. *Remedial and Special Education, 17, 1,* 48–58.

Wolf, M., & Bowers, P. G. (1999). The double-deficit hypothesis for the developmental dyslexias. *Journal of Educational Psychology, 91,* 415–438.

Yetter, B. D. (2001). Weave spelling through the day. *Teaching Pre-K–8. 32, 3,* 50–51.

Zutell, J. (1998). Word sorting: A developmental spelling approach to word study for delayed readers. *Reading and Writing Quarterly, 14, 2,* 219–238.

Index

Main entries in **bold**

affective aspects of spelling 42, 63
alliteration **13**
alphabetic principle **10**, **12**, 13, **47**
analogy as a spelling strategy **16**, 23, 24, **26**, 27, **30**, 38, 42, 51, 53
assessment **72–79**
  diagnostic 72, 73, **77–78**
  formal 72, 74, **77**
  formative **73**
  informal 74, **77**
  methods of **74–79**
  norm referenced 73–74
  summative **73**
assistive technology 34, **43–44**, 65
auditory analysis **13**, 14
auditory discrimination **13**, 14
automaticity **19**, **24**, 38

base words **16–17**, **31**, 42, 85
Benchmarks for Literacy **5**, 9, 36, 45, 73

checking spelling 11, 12, **21**, 23, 24, **26**, 28, 29, 30, **38**, 41, 42, 46, **55–56**, 75, 79
cognitive components of spelling 7, **60**
computer-assisted learning 40, 43, **44**, **45**, 63
constant time delay (CTD) **45**
core spelling vocabulary 36, **38**, **41**, **56–57**, 81
cross-curricular aspects of spelling **35**, 41

curriculum guidelines 5, 7, **36**
curriculum-based testing **77**

deafness 14
demonstration **54**
  as a teaching tactic 31, 54, **55**, 63, 64
developmental aspects of spelling 8, **21–23**, 33, 36, 37, 40, **52**, 62, 65, 73
diagnostic assessment 72, 73, **77–78**
diagnostic interview 74, **78**
dictation 31, **52–53**, 58
differentiation of spelling instruction 8, 40, **52**, 56, 65
direct teaching 5, 6, 29
  see also explicit instruction
Directed Spelling Thinking Activity (DSTA) **52**
dynamic assessment 78
dyslexia 14, **62**
dysorthographia 59, **62**

Early Literacy In-service Course (ELIC) 4
English: A curriculum profile for Australian schools 5, 36, 73
English as a second language 6, 7, 52
error analysis **75–76**
error correction 46, **55–56**, 64, **65–66**
error modelling **64**, 65
explicit instruction 4, **5**, 6, 19, **31**, 38, 42, **47**, **53-54**, 61, **63**, **64**, 69

feedback from teacher 2, 4, 19, **35**, 39, 40, 42, 45, 54, **63**, 64, 72, 78

101

flashcard 57
Fonetik Spelling 29, 65, **67–68**

guided practice 35, 39, 45, 54, 79

handwriting 10, **19–20**, 43, 67
high-frequency words **12**, **56–57**, 60, 63, **81**

incidental learning vii, 22, 34, 47, 63
International English Spelling Assessment 80
intervention methods 29, **63–70**, 76
invented spelling 2, **14**, **22–23**, **42**, 47, 66, 73
investigative approach **43**, 50, 52
irregular words 6, 12, 17, 23, **29**, 32, **57**, 67, **68**, 76, 81

keyboarding 11, 19, **43–44**, 63, 64, 66

learning difficulties 6–7, 8, 11, **13–14**, 31, 37, 41, **44**, 45, 59, 60, **62**, 64, **65**, 71, 75, 79
learning disability 44, 59, **62**
letter-to-sound correspondences
  see sound-to-symbol relationships
lexical memory **11**, 14, 24
lists for spelling 2, **8**, 35, **37–38**, **41**, **45**, 52, 56, 76, 77, 80
literacy hour 5, 39
look-say-cover-write-check strategy **29–30**, 54, 64, 65, 70

memorisation 2, 8, 11, 28, **37**, 61
mini lessons **37**, 40
mnemonics 26, **32**, 53
morphemic principles 14, **16–17**, **31**, 38, 50, 54, 55, **61**
morphographs **16**, 17, 20, 39
morphology **16–17**, 31

motor memory **19**
multisensory approaches 57, 63, 64, **70**
multisyllabic words 68, 75, 76

National Literacy Plan 5
National Literacy Strategy (UK) 5, 20, 37, 39, 45
national testing 5
natural learning **4**, 6, 7
neuro-linguistic programming (NLP) 69

observation of students' skills 26, **74**
old way – new way **65–66**
onset and rime **13**, **48–49**
organising spelling instruction 36, **37–41**, **70**
orthographic awareness **10**, 14, **15–16**
orthographic processing 60, 62
orthographic units 12, 13, **15–16**, 19, **23–24**, 30, 38, 46, **48–49**, **50**, 60, 76, **84**
over-enunciation as a spelling strategy **27**, 28, **31**, 32, 53
overlapping waves theory **25–26**

parents 1, 2, 7, 39
parents' concerns **1–2**
peer tutoring 40, 64, **70**, 71
perceptual skills in spelling 7, 10, **11–15**, 22, 59, **60**, 69
phoneme blending **13**, 46, 49
phonemes 8, 10, **12**, 13, 21, 26, 47, 64, 79
phonetic alternatives **15**, **76**
phonetic stage of spelling 12, **22–23**, 60, 61
phonic analysis 76
phonic knowledge **5**, 10, **14**, 15, 26, **47–48**, 49, 56, 61, 68, 76
phonic skills 18, **47–48**
phonic strategies for spelling **28–29**, 67

INDEX

phonics
  teaching of 20, **47–51**
phonological awareness 10, **12–15**, 28, 61, 62
policy documents
  government 1, **5**, 7, 9, 36
  school-based 7, **34**, **35**
portfolios 75
practice
  importance of 7, 15, **42**, **54**, 63, 64, 69
prefixes 16, 17, 27, 31
pre-phonemic stage of spelling **22**, 62
pre-service teacher education vii, 6, **8**
primary schools 36, 46
  spelling instruction **36–39**, 40
proactive interference 65
pronunciation
  its role in spelling 13, 16, 26, **27**, 31, **75**
proofreading 11, 24, 26, 30, 38, 41, 46, 53, **55–56**

reading experience
  its role in spelling 10, 15, **17–19**, 24, 47, 50, **59**, 63
recitation (letter rehearsal) **32**, 54, 61
repeated writing 12, 26, **56**, 57, 65, **66–67**, 81
research on spelling 6–7, 16, 28–31, 41, **64–65**
reversal of letters 60
rhyming **13**, 85
rote learning 25, 28, 34, 39, 61
  see also memorisation
rules in spelling 8, 11, 15, **16**, 24, 26, 27, 32, 42, 46, 50, 51, 64

secondary schools 19, 32, 35, 36, 68
  spelling instruction 35, **41**
segmentation **13**, 42, 48, 76
self-assessment in spelling **78–79**, 80

self-correction 21, 38, 41, 52, 53, **55**, 74, 75
self-directing strategy **30**
sequential motor memory 19
simultaneous oral spelling (SOS) 32, 65, **68–69**
sounding out
  as a spelling strategy 12, **26**, **27**, 79
sound-to-symbol relationships 14, 15, 29, 36, **47–48**, 61, 68
  see also phonic knowledge
spell it as it sounds strategy **28–29**, 67
spell-checkers 11, 30, 41, **43**, **44**, 65, **67**, 78, 79
spelling
  assessment of **72–79**
  cross-curricular aspects **35**
  developmental stages **21–24**, 37
  difficulties with 14, **59–62**
  importance of **5**, 35
  public concerns about **2–4**
  standards in **3–4**, **5**, 9
  sub-skills **11–17**
  teaching of **5**, **7**, 9, 26, **28–32**, **36–39**, **47–55**
spelling by analogy **16**, 23, **26**, 27, **30**, 38, 53
spelling demons 15, 53, 76, 79
Spelling Mastery 2007 **17**, **20**
spelling pronunciation **27**, 31
Spelling Recovery 76, 98
Spelling through morphographs 17, 20, 39, 90
standardised testing 36, 73
standards in spelling **3–4**, **5**, 8, **9**, 45
strategies for spelling **25–28**, **65–70**, 79
  examples of 24–25, **26–27**, **28–32**
  teaching of 19, **38–39**, **53–55**
suffixes 27, **31**, 61, 80
syllables 10, 13, 22, 28, 29, 30, 38, 54, 67, 76
synthetic phonics **47**

teacher education 4, 6, **8**
  inadequate coverage of teaching spelling vii, 1, 5, **6**, **7**
teacher-made tests 77, 78
teachers **8**, 26, 31, 34, 35, 41, 42, 63
  their concerns **1–2**, **34–35**, 36, 37, 39
  their lack of expertise vii, 6, 7, **8**, **17**
testing 2, 5, 72, 73, **77–78**
THRASS 39, 47, **58**
time allocation for teaching spelling 34, **39–40**
transitional stage of spelling 12, **23–24**
transposition of letters 60, 75
trends in spelling instruction vii, **1–4**, **6**
typing 19, 44, 57, **66**
  see also keyboarding

visual imagery 23, 26, **27**, **29**, 38, 53, 60, **69**

visual memory **11–12**, 29, 57, 60, 61, **69**
visualisation **69**

whole class teaching 37, **40**, 76
whole-language approach vii, **3–4**, 5, 6–7, 37, 39, 69, 72
whole-word spelling strategy **12**, 31, 57, 67
word building **48–49**, 84
word endings 61, 75
word families 15, 30, 38, 42, **48–49**, **50–51**, 64, **85**
word processors 43, 44, 63, 65
word recognition 17, 18, 46, 47
word sorting 15, 50, **51–52**, 65, **86**
word study 7, 39, 41, **49**, 57, 61, 63
  activities for 30, **49–52**, 57, 76
  importance of 5, 7, 19, 39
work samples 74, **75**